Nathan Bangs:
The Architect of
American Methodism

DANIEL F. FLORES, PH.D.

ISBN: 1517702844
ISBN-13: 978-1517702847

DEDICATION

For all who dare answer the Holy Spirit's call to lead the people of God.

CONTENTS

AUTHOR'S PREFACE

In late January of 1859, somewhere between two and three hundred people gathered at the home of the Rev. Dr. McClintock in New York City. From there they proceeded to a house in Irving Place where they surprised Rev. Dr. Nathan Bangs and his family. Bishop Janes brought the crowd to order and made preliminary remarks before turning proceedings over to Dr. Carlton of the Methodist Book Concern. The prologue to his formal address appears below.

> Rev. Dr. Bangs, permit me to assure you that the company here assembled are your warm and devoted friends, and as such, most heartily and cordially covered in the sentiments of our worthy and expert Bishop. Many have known you from our childhood, and we learned to venerate and respect you in early life. For years we have listened to your instructions from the pulpit, and greatly to our profit we have read your books and other productions of your pen; and now, Sir, after a long life of labor and toil as a faithful and devoted minister of the Lord Jesus Christ, we thought it but fitting and proper to present you a trifling testimony of our personal respect.[1]

His friends then presented him with a fine walking cane filled with four hundred five dollar gold coins, a splendid symbol of his many contributions to the organization and leadership of The Methodist Episcopal Church in America. Today the golden cane would easily be worth a million US dollars. More to be desired than gold are his legacy of passionate worship and his love of sound Wesleyan theology.

I was very fortunate to have been appointed graduate assistant to Dr. Kenneth E. Rowe, Methodist Librarian and my dissertation advisor. In the course of my daily duties, I encountered numerous references to Nathan Bangs in the antique books and early conference minutes of the Methodist Episcopal Church. He was everywhere in the archives, but strangely absent from history books. I could not understand why someone so prominent in establishing the church had been relegated to a footnote here and there. I made a long-term commitment to seek out the missing pieces of the jigsaw puzzle of American Methodism with Bangs being my major lead. My research led me down labyrinths laden with many onerous, dense tomes on British and American religious history. At length, I was led to the conclusion that Nathan Bangs was indeed the key to understanding the post-Asbury Wesleyan movement in America.

At first, I chose not to publish my dissertation because of my own distaste for "dry as dust" dissertations. More importantly, I expected a bright scholar to emerge with improvements on my thesis. After a decade of reviewing the new literature, many excellent studies have been published on the grand topic of American Methodism, though Bangs is rarely mentioned. Aside from the pale obelisk marking his grave and a stained glass chapel window hidden in the bowels of Wesleyan University, I have not found any three dimensional artifacts of permanence preserving his noble likeness. Nor have I discovered any church, school, or society bearing his name. Yet, I believe Nathan Bangs was as important a figure in American Methodist history as Asbury, Coke, Emory, and McKendree. Many of his most significant contributions are still with us in the United Methodist Church and related Wesleyan denominations. I finally decided to publish portions of my research to supplement reading material for my seminary students. For my United Methodist history class at Perkins School of Theology, I chose portions on Bangs' leadership role in developing the Methodist Episcopal Church. This first book was published under the title *Sacrificial Leadership: Nathan Bangs and the transformation of the Wesleyan Movement in* America. It was clear to me that a second installment would be necessary to meet the needs of my students of the Wesleyan Heritage course for the Regional Course of Study School. This latest publication, *Nathan Bangs: Architect of American Methodism,* focuses on the social structures that propped the spiritual life of the early movement. Both books include chapters on preaching which was a hallmark of American Methodist culture. After nearly twenty years of ministry, I still hold the conviction that an historical study of our spiritual heritage can serve as a stimulus to revival. At the bare minimum, it can instruct us what our forebears thought constituted being an authentic "Wesleyan."

Soli Deo Gloria!

1 REVIVALISM

"Methodist," said I; "what's that? What sort of people are they?"

"Ah," said he, "they are the strangest people you ever saw; they shout and halloo so loud you may hear them for miles; they hold that all will be saved, and a man can live without sin in this life and yet that a Christian can fall from grace...."[2]

In spite of the MEC's gains in respectability, middle class Methodists still grimaced on the unhappy occasion when one of their country preachers wandered into town dressed in his black Quaker-style outfit. No less embarrassing was the corybantic worship style of rural Methodists. The infamous circuit rider Peter Cartwright was not ashamed to admit he was a "shouting Methodist." In the early years, the MEC was largely identified as a revivalist movement. As such, Methodists and their constituent members prized enthusiastic worship, vital piety, and perfectionist doctrine. Their informal mode of worship extended beyond the local circuits to broader fields of missions. Camp meetings were the populist arena for religious expression and the seed bed for popular piety. There the "practical and experimental divinity" of the Wesleys found unlikely bedfellows with the rustic maxims of the brush arbor revivalists. The result was an odd blending of sacred hymns and nostalgic choruses. As a byproduct, Methodist meetings were also known as venues for public displays of emotion and religious fanaticism.

Earlier, Bishop Francis Asbury's army of circuit riders disseminated the Wesleyan message of holiness wherever they lighted. The popularity of David Brainerd's missionary diary lured Methodist missionaries to the far reaches of the frontier. Rural Methodist chapels depended on traveling preachers to nurture and feed them according to their place on the circuit. Circuit riders had the additional burden of organizing stations into new chapels. These points were often used to hold evangelistic worship services in the mode of camp meetings. From Long Island to the Western Reserve, Methodist preachers used camp meetings to evangelize *en masse*. New churches that formed out of these campaigns were able to "sustain and routinize the socializing power of the camp meeting."[3] By the mid-nineteenth century, the evangelistic successes of the MEC reached deep into the fast moving socialite scenes of city life. Backwoods Methodist preachers, legendary for their plain form of preaching and singing, became an oddity in urban America.

The movement towards respectability exerted tectonic pressure on the social structure of the local church often resulting in white-hot friction between the generations. Changes in class in turn affected the preferred oratory worship styles of the local congregation. By 1832, it was plain that the MEC's in New York City were becoming more "church-like." They demanded educated clergy to lead more formalized Sunday services. Churches were being pulled away from the idea of circuit preachers and implemented the concept of a "settled pastorate."[4] Nathan Bangs, one of the first of these settled pastors, experienced first-hand the change. The occasional incursions of ecstatic behavior into churches grated hard on the up and coming Methodists. As Bangs demonstrated at New York's John Street Church, the spirits of these prophets were subject to Methodist discipline.

> His [Bangs'] ability in the pulpit attracted the people in crowds at his numerous appointments, for his word was in "demonstration of the Spirit and of power."
>
> ...If not intellectually polished, he was intellectually powerful; a certain mightiness of thought and feeling bore down at times all before him, especially when he preached to large assemblies at quarterly and camp-meetings. At one of the latter it was estimated that two hundred hearers were awakened under a single sermon; they fell, like wounded men, on the right and on the left; he preached on for two hours; and it is said that an

3

earthquake, shaking the camp throughout those awful
hours, could hardly have produced a more irresistible
excitement.[5]

Preaching has always been the central element in Protestant
worship. Early American Methodism was no exception. John Wesley
suggested that preaching Gospel and Law should be in this order. "At
our first beginning to preach at any place, after a general declaration of the
love of God to sinners, and his willingness that they should be saved, to
preach the law, in the strongest, the closest, the most searching manner
possible; only intermixing the gospel here and there, and showing if, as it
were, afar off."[6]   After Wesley, early Methodist preachers disregarded
exegetical accuracy in favor of inflaming "stone-cold hearts" and
rekindling "the lukewarm by the power of the gospel, through the agency
of the Holy Spirit."[7] Nathan Bangs method of evangelistic preaching
relied on the power of the Spirit and human reason. His presentation
style marked him as "a master of theology and logic, and better known
among the sects than almost any Methodist preacher, except Asbury."[8]

The Methodist emphasis on evangelistic preaching was by no
means confined to the venue of the local chapel. Rather, it became the

preferred mode for communicating to the masses at public gatherings such as camp meetings and quarterly meetings. The technique of calling sinners to repentance was refined in the emotional smelting pots of camp meetings. This informal mode of religious gathering was especially popular in rural areas, although it was not an exclusively rural phenomenon. It flourished so widely that it is difficult to separate camp meetings from American Methodist piety. They became most popular during the liminal period between the Great Awakening and the Second Great Awakening.[9] Such gatherings produced an environment where evangelistic preaching was highly effective. Therefore, they became the preferred and well-worn tool by which Methodists extended and sustained the effects of the Second Great Awakening.[10] The camp meeting was already an institution by the time Nathan Bangs entered national prominence. Samuel Kennerly reported to Bangs of the visible effectiveness of camp meetings for mass evangelism.

> On the last morning of the meeting, we called up the penitents to pray with them for the last time at that place, and there were about thirty who came forward; five and twenty of them were males, and some of the first families in that country. The second camp-meeting also appeared to commence, progress and end, under the superintendence of the Most High. It is thought

5

that a least one hundred souls were raised from a death of sin to a life of righteousness, at this meeting, the most of whom were young men of respectability. It was observed that in general their struggle for redemption was much more severe than usual, and the evidence of their acceptance much clearer than common.[11]

Methodist camp meetings originated from three separate traditions: Methodist, Scottish Reformed, and Quaker. The Methodist roots can be traced to the open air preaching of George Whitefield, John Wesley, and Charles Wesley. Methodist preachers were often not welcome in Church of England pulpits, despite the fact that the Wesleys and Whitefield were ordained Anglican ministers.[12] John Wesley first preached outdoors when he was put out of his father's church at Epworth. The well-known engraving by George Washington Brownlow illustrates Wesley preaching from atop his father's tombstone outside St. Andrew's Church.[13] This exercise was distinct from his later experiences of field preaching because the former was on sanctified ground. George Whitefield encouraged Wesley to emulate his own successes by field preaching to the poor colliers at Hanham Mount near Kingswood. A well-rehearsed description of this first open air preaching is quite dramatic. "The first discovery of their being affected was to see the white gutters made by their tears, which plentifully fell down their black cheeks as they came out of their coal pits."[14]   Wesley, convince of the efficacy of field preaching, thereafter "submitted to be more vile" by following Whitefield's example.

Charles Wesley also had some first-hand experience with preaching in the open air style at Thaxted (or Thackstead) at the invitation of some Quakers.[15] "Many Quakers, and near seven hundred others, attended, while I declared in the highways, 'the Scripture hath concluded all under sin.'"[16] Shortly afterwards Charles preached from a tomb stone when put out of his Islington parish.[17] The three evangelists regularly preached at Hanham Mount and the "brickyards" and the "bowling green" in Bristol. Thus, they established open air preaching as a normal aspect of Methodist ministry.[18] Whitefield later carried his method of open air preaching to America. His masterful technique even drew the attention of Benjamin Franklin.[19]

There was another tradition exported to America known as the Scottish "sacramental seasons."   This tradition was also called "communion seasons" or "holy fairs."[20]   During the Scottish

Reformation, the Ulster-Scots, or Scotch-Irish, developed an open air service, a formal ancestor of the informal camp meeting. These religious gatherings were held in outlying areas to meet the sacramental needs of rural folk. They were marked by periods of fasting and reflection. This annual or biannual event would continue for a matter of days before culminating in celebration of the Lord's Supper in the outdoors.[21]

George Whitefield reportedly preached to over thirty-thousand people at the famed "Cambuslang Wark" in 1742.[22] Furthermore, he made at least fourteen trips to Scotland during his career, often participating in the sacramental seasons.[23]

> Last Lord's day, I preached in the morning, in the park at Edinburgh, to a great multitude. Afterwards, I attended, and partook of the holy sacrament, and served four tables. In the afternoon, I preached in the churchyard, to a far greater number. Such a passover, I never saw before.[24]

Although John Wesley made as many as twenty-two visits to Scotland, he was not impressed by the Scottish form of communion. "How much more simple, as well as more solemn, is the service of the Church of England."[25] Wesley's preference for the Anglican sacramental

8

ritual prevented him from adopting the Scottish service for his Wesleyan preachers.

The Scottish tradition entered America by way of the Scottish and Ulster-Scot Presbyterian immigrants. Enclaves of Presbyterian immigrants almost immediately staged sacramental occasions fully reminiscent of Scotland and Ulster.[26] The most famous of these immigrants was James McGready. He experienced success holding the sacramental season eighteen times from 1797 to 1800.[27] Shortly thereafter, he joined Barton W. Stone, another Presbyterian, in organizing teams of Presbyterian, Methodist, and Baptist preachers for a meeting at Cane Ridge. Elements reminiscent of the sacramental season such as the action sermon, table service, and plurality of ministers were evident at Cane Ridge.[28] Presbyterians, Baptists, and Methodists participated in the event together creating a nonsectarian atmosphere. Consider the utopian account offered by Levi Purviance.

> This was not a sectarian meeting, although it was held at a Presbyterian meeting house. Baptist, Methodist, and Presbyterians were simultaneously engaged. Perfect friendship, unanimity, and brotherly kindness prevailed. They had come together, to the help of the Lord against the mighty, and "Zion was terrible as an army with banners." The meeting lasted six

days; the last sermon that was delivered on the occasion was by a Methodist preacher, by the name of Samuel Hitt. It is known only to God how many were converted at this meeting. There were no means by which even to ascertain how many professed religion. The object of the meeting was not to build up any sect or party, but to bring sinners to the Savior.[29]

From the enterprising evangelist's perspective, camp meetings were the perfect method of evangelism. They created an atmosphere where worship appealed to the heart, Christian virtues were profound, and resistance to conversion was diminished. Barton Stone was so effected by the catholicity of Cane Ridge that he defected from Presbyterianism. Stone later joined Alexander Campbell in founding the restorationist group known as the Christian Church or Disciples of Christ. Fifty years afterwards, Stone recollected Cane Ridge as a fruitful revival, though mixed with fanaticism.

Having heard of a remarkable religious excitement in the south of Kentucky, and in Tennessee, under the labors of James McGready and other Presbyterian ministers, I was very anxious to be among them; and, early in the spring of 1801, went there to attend a camp-meeting...The scene to me was new, and passing strange. It baffled description. Many, very many fell down, as men slain in battle, and continued for hours together in an apparently breathless and motionless state – sometimes for a few moments reviving, and exhibiting symptoms of life by a deep groan, or piercing shriek, or by a prayer for mercy most fervently uttered. After lying thus for hours, they obtained deliverance. The gloomy cloud, which had covered their faces, seemed gradually and visibly to disappear, and hope in smiles brightened into joy – they would rise shouting deliverance, and then would address the surrounding multitude in language truly eloquent and impressive.[30]

Nathan Bangs appreciated the spirit of catholicity prevalent in camp meetings. He was also well aware of its historical connection to the Reformed tradition. As mentioned above, Bangs was rarely known to put aside his strong prejudices against Calvinists. Yet, he was willing to overlook the Reformed connection to camp meetings for the promise of spiritual blessings. In this instance, he was a true Wesleyan pragmatist. On the other hand, Bangs had no qualms about writing camp meetings into Methodist history and tradition.

> It will be seen by the preceding remarks that these camp meetings were not the result of a previously digested plan, but like every other peculiarity of Methodism, were introduced by providential occurrences, and were embraced and followed up by God's servants because they found them subservient to the grand design they had in view, namely, the salvation of the world by Jesus Christ. Indeed, they did not originate with the Methodists, but upon a sacramental

occasion among the Presbyterians, at which time there
was such a remarkable outpouring of the Divine Spirit
in the people as inclined them to protract their
exercises to an unusual period; and then this being
noised abroad brought others to the place, and finally
so many that no house could hold them; this induced
them to go into the field, and erect temporary shelters
for themselves, and to bring provision for their
sustenance; and finding God so abundantly blessed
them in these meetings, they were led to continue
them, until they at length became very general among
the Methodists throughout the country.[31]

Initially, the Presbyterians, like other groups, received numerous

converts from camp meetings. However, Presbyterians were less at ease

with the disorderly conduct also associated with these gatherings.

Furthermore, they were not reticent to express publicly their

disenchantment. In 1805, the General Assembly denounced camp

meetings on the grounds that, "God is a God of order and not of

confusion, and whatever tends to destroy the comely order of his worship

is not from him."[32] The earlier form Scottish Reform communion

festivals had peaked in significance for American religious history by

1815.[33] A similar fate was falling on camp meetings in England. Lay

preachers Hugh Bourne and William Clowes invited the eccentric

American lay evangelist Lorenzo Dow to organize an American style camp meeting. The first English camp meeting was held at a hill called Mow Cop on May 31, 1807. The Wesleyan Conference feared the camp meetings were havens for violent emotionalism, sexual promiscuity, and seditious activity.[34] Later that year, they officially condemned camp meetings.

> It is our judgment, that even supposing such meetings to be allowable in America, they are highly improper in England, and likely to be productive of considerable mischief. And we disclaim all connexion with them.[35]

Hugh Bourne, beloved for his peripatetic lay preaching, was expelled from the Wesleyans in 1808 on the flimsy grounds that he missed a class meeting. This was a serious offense according to the class rules. However, Bourne and Clowes continued to promote camp meetings under the aegis of their newly formed Society of Primitive Methodists, 1810.[36]

American Methodists had no trouble accommodating the Spirit-filled religion of the camp meeting. It engendered a receptive mood for evangelism and renewal. It was so well received that it practically became a means of grace among American Methodists.

In 1748, the British itinerant John Bennet scheduled quarterly meetings for two circuits. The success of this experiment caught John Wesley's attention. He decided to adopt this Quaker tradition rather than the Scottish Reform tradition. At the 1749 Annual Conference, Wesley appointed Bennet to instruct his preachers in mandatory quarterly meetings.[37] Bishop Asbury adopted the camp meeting as an expansion of the quarterly meeting.[38] The quarterly meeting insured a certain regularity for camp meetings. The importance of quarterly meetings as a venue for Methodist worship began to fade in 1802, so that camp meetings dominated the scene by 1812.[39] The quarterly meetings were still important for administrative purposes, but the camp meetings took over the "liturgical and evangelistic aspects" of American Methodism.[40] The early Methodist camp meetings were considered liturgical because they included communion as part of the service.[41]

In 1805, Henry Ryan and William Case introduced camp meetings to Canada while Nathan Bangs was still a missionary there.[42] As an added benefit, the extended worship services brought spiritual refreshment for weary Canadian itinerants. Bangs reported an instance of personal renewal as a result of these services. "Great was the good that followed...I returned to Augusta Circuit and renewed my labors, somewhat worn, but full of faith and the Holy Ghost."[43] Bangs was very successful in utilizing camp meetings and quarterly meetings to plant new congregations in his circuit. At his eulogy, Bishop Edmund Storer Janes would remark on this aspect of Bangs' ministry in the Rhinebeck District (ca. 1813).

> Dr. Bangs was then at the maturity of his manhood. His preaching was powerful; his quarterly meetings and camp-meetings were jubilatic [sic] occasions, crowded by multitudes from many miles around. He traversed his vast district a son of thunder, and before he left it was begun that zealous provision of chapels and parsonages which has dotted the whole region with Methodist edifices--a chapel and a preacher's house in almost every village.[44]

A century later, Joseph Edward Sanderson judged Canadian camp meetings as having "harmonized with the earnest, evangelizing spirit of Methodism and proved mightily effective in awakening and arousing whole communities."[45] Francis Asbury was solidly convinced of the camp meeting's usefulness in evangelism. This is evident from his journal entry

15

dated 24 September 1808. "I rejoice to think there will be perhaps four or five hundred camp-meetings this year; may this year outdo all former years in the conversion of precious souls to God! Work, Lord, for this own honour [*sic*] and glory!"[46] Nathan Bangs credited the massive growth of the MEC to camp meetings. "If the Methodist Church in America has increased beyond any parallel during one fourth of a century past, we must ascribe much of her spiritual prosperity, under God, to the blessed influence of such meetings."[47]

The main criticism of American Presbyterians and British Wesleyans against camp meetings was that they elicited emotional and unruly behavior. Unquestionably, there were ample reports of emotionalism and motor phenomena. Excitement was manifested vocally as "a sudden burst of the groans, shrieks, and cries of sinners, and acclamations of joy and shouts of Christians."[48] Nathan Bangs reported having personally experienced physical evidence of affective religion when he was preaching at a camp meeting in Canada.

> At midnight, on the last night, while an indescribable sense of the divine presence prevailed throughout the encampment, he stood on a log and exhorted the people with overwhelming effect, his powerful voice

reverberating over the ground and through the woods. While stretching out his arms, as if to bless the weeping multitude, they stiffened and remained extended, and for some time he stood thus addressing the hearers, weeping with them that wept. He was at last led to a tent, but with still extended arms. The strange effect continued there, but did not disturb his religious joy. "I was continually uttering praise; the tent was soon crowded, and at a single utterance the whole group fell to the ground…

    'O'erwhelmed with His stupendous grace

    They did not in His presence move:

    But breathed unutterable praise

    In rapturous awe and silent love.'

…[I felt] a prickling sensation over the whole body, like that felt when a limb is said to be asleep; but this was followed by a soft, soothing feeling, as if I were anointed with oil, and such a consciousness of the presence and peace of God pervaded me as I cannot describe."[49]

Despite numerous critiques against religious fanaticism, camp meetings thrived as the preferred venue for evangelistic preaching for many years. Their popularity was their simple and effective means of generating new recruits.[50] On the other hand, evangelistic preaching styles most associated with emotional outbursts did not easily cross over into congregational settings. A "widening gulf" formed between expressions of camp meeting religion and structure of church religion.[51] Consequently, evangelistic preaching, associated with camp meetings, become less prominent in the local church.

Rev. Dr. Nathan Bangs portrayed as a dashing preacher. Bangs had an unusual vocal quality that was described as a "double voice." With his neck constantly fixed at an odd angle, due to congenital torticollis, Bangs kept his listeners spellbound.

2 PULPIT PRINCES

The revival for the first fortnight was rapid in its spread – glorious in its progress...To forcible and energetic exhortations our pastors added the precepts and doctrines of practical and experimental religion – while polemical divinity and disputes concerning non-essentials (those bulwarks on which bigotry erects her throne, and from which she hurls her anathemas) were as much as possible avoided.[52]

Converts of revivals were usually funneled into classes where they would be taught doctrine in the Methodist tradition. Preaching didactic sermons bypassed the process. As local congregations became more important, evangelistic preaching lost prominence.[53] The camp meeting demanded evangelistic fervor. Settled congregation demanded education in the pulpits and in the pews.

Abel Stevens noted that the former preachers "came out from the people, and knew how to address the people; and the popular effects of their preaching, the great massive in-gatherings of the people into their communion, are a demonstration of their power nothing short of magnificent."[54] The induction of ministerial candidates into seminaries received criticism for removing students from real life situations and isolating them in cloisters of theological education.[55] The importance of teaching, rather than converting, was instilled into the young preachers. This emphasis may be traced to the practice of using class meetings as a follow-up to mass evangelism. Have just returned from Camp-meeting held at Compo. It was a time of God's power; many were converted, many reclaimed, many sanctified. Glory be to God--to His name be praise forever and ever! We had a trial of our faith, being detained by a terrible storm from Friday until Monday noon. We continued our meetings, and about thirty were converted during the storm. I took sixteen from this place into Class.[56]

In the quote above, Heman Bangs confirmed that converts resulting from camp meetings were channeled into Methodist class meetings. Class meetings took new converts and quickly mainstreamed them into the system. Their simple, but organized structure created a new subgroup apart from the normal social order. The genius of the class meeting was its inner and outer experience of living discipleship and grace.[57] However, it could not keep pace with the momentum of the social upheaval at this time. Lack of accountability and a dry formalism were blamed for low attendance and defunct classes.[58] The class leader functioned as a lay pastor who was expected to exhort class members in the absence of a preacher. The availability of "stationed ministers" not only eliminated circuits, but it also diminished the role of the class leader.[59] The class meeting faded as the MEC was divided between camp meeting religion and the liturgically based church religion. Consequently, the more formal churches directed resources into mission societies and service groups.[60] The didactic emphasis naturally carried over into preaching by the settled ministers.

Let us not think, then, that we require in our large cities only educated and polished preachers and restricted modes of labor; these we must have, but we get need these, as much as if not more than in the first days of Methodism, voices "crying in the wilderness, Prepare ye the way of the Lord" – men who will "circuit" these cities as did our fathers, and, like them, preach continually and powerfully the primary truths of religion among the neglected populace.[61]

Upwardly mobile Methodists demanded educated preachers with a mastery of elocution. But they still wanted substance in the message. The senior Methodists, represented by figures such as James Quinn, a pioneer preacher from Ohio, reluctantly acknowledged the demand. However, they regarded it with suspicion in the work of the preaching ministry.

Well, now, I think that this plain, Scriptural, common-sense kind of preaching, goes very well; and with intelligent, well-informed men, I know many that greatly prefer it; and as to those who only *think* themselves intelligent, or wise, perhaps there is as little hope of them now as there was in the days of Solomon; and, may be, St. Paul would tell them that they must become fools, that they may become wise.[62]

Those preachers who graduated from the so-called "Brush College" of mentored ministry did not have the advantages belonging to Course of Study trained ministers. Between 1830 and 1858, the list included as preaching instruction *Preacher's Manual*, by Adam Clarke, and *Rhetoric*, by Alexander Jamieson. These were replaced in 1858 by *Identifier*, by Nicholas Snethen.[63]

Those outside the bounds of Course of Study could avail themselves of short articles on preaching reprinted and serialized in MEC publications. The availability of these resources facilitated continuing education for active ministers in the field, regardless of age or experience. In 1828, John Wesley's "Thoughts on Preaching the Gospel " was reprinted in the *Methodist Review* as an aid to young preachers. In the article, Wesley stated that the three emphases of preaching as doctrine, salvation, and experience.[64] Nathan Bangs focused more on the attitude and carriage of the preaching task. In his serialized *Letters to Young Ministers of the Gospel*, Bangs offered seven keys to oratory success.

> Well, then, first study yourself. 2. Understand your subject. 3. Feel its importance. 4. Keep master of yourself – that is, be not depressed by timidity, nor swoln [sic] with self-confidence and vanity. 5. While you derive all the knowledge you can from every source, and especially from all you hear and read, make no efforts to imitate any man, neither in his gestures, the intonations of his voice, nor the peculiar enunciation of his words. 6. Set God always before you; and as if standing upon the threshold of eternity, labour [sic] as though this might be your last effort to save those who now hear you. And if you must have artificial helps, study Blair, Campbell, Maury, Knox, and Wesley. But, above all, if you would succeed in accomplishing the all-important end of your mission, be most solicitous for the holy anointing.[65]

Bangs' suggestions were very much in Wesley's tradition of pairing together knowledge and vital piety. His published advice to "Junior Preacher" to be a "serious and solemn" deportment meant that preaching was not a craft to be trifled with. Rather, it was a labour [sic] for God."[66] This was a way of teaching the congregation, by example, that preaching was sacred speech, not merely human oratory to be mimicked.

William Jay's lectures taught that didactic preaching offered the potential to lift up a congregation beyond their own level on knowledge. Such preaching was not only admonished, it was considered a duty to the uneducated.

> Now a preacher need not grovel down to the lowest level of the vulgar; yea, he should always take his aim a little above them, in order to raise and improve their taste: but he must not soar out of their sight and reach. He yet may be tempted to this by the presence of others. But let him remember, that those who are more educated and refined, ought not only to endure but to commend his accommodation; – yea, and they will commend instead of censuring him, if they are really concerned for the welfare of their brethren less privileged than themselves.[67]

Thomas Maddin was not as happy with the developments of Methodist preaching in the 1850s. He lamented that some preachers left behind the fiery form of piety of "Young Methodism" for a "form without the power of godliness." In his exposé of an unidentified "Mr. R," he cited several unfavorable characteristics of the gentlemanly, though apostate, Methodist preacher.

> His congregations were of the *élite*. His discourses were of the popular character. His position might be regarded as by the would-be-great, for though there were but too evidently the marks of deterioration of his piety, there were none of his popularity. His sermons were fine specimens of cultivated intellect, finely arranged, naturally connected, logically argued, rhetorically polished, and sonorously delivered.[68]

Mr. R stood in quite a contrast to the earlier descriptions of Cartwright and Bangs. Cartwright possessed none of the polish, but depended on spiritual fervor. Bangs achieved eloquence, but maintained his appreciation of religious fervor, though in controlled measures. A. Vinet, the nineteenth century French homiletics professor taught preachers that instructing doctrine was the end of pulpit eloquence. "The preacher's chief business is instruction; this is the basis of his work; exhortation, reproof, sharpens his teaching, but it is always teaching."[69] In fact, didactic preaching created a tendency to be more uniform in emphasis by keeping Methodist doctrine central. Polemical preaching, more popular in Bangs' early ministry, was de-emphasized where Methodism became more respectable.[70] On the other hand, after 1858 the General Conference added polemical doctrinal works defending Methodist history and ecclesiology to the course of study reading list.[71]

> I have heard sermons in which the essentials of the gospel were scarcely touched. Should the preacher have a propensity to display his oratory, and be anxious to turn his periods handsomely, at least his application should be pungent, pointed, and to the purpose. The designs of preaching is to awaken sinners, and to bring them to Christ; – to urge believers to the attainment of holiness of heart and life; – to show sinners the turpitude of their hearts and sinfulness of their practice, and to bring them to the foot of the cross, stripped of self and of all self dependence; – to press the old Methodistical doctrines by faith; the direct evidence from God, through faith in the merits of Christ, of the forgiveness of sin; and the adoption into his family. Nor are we to be ashamed of that unfashionable doctrine, Christian perfection: – but we should point out clearly a travail of soul, not only for justification, but for sanctification, and the evidence of it.[72]

As early as 1827, Freeborn Garrettson could already detect a shift in the emphasis of many preachers. His preaching was described as "entertaining and useful" devoid of "a dry detail of uninteresting matter, or with speculations which did not profit the hearer."[73] Such interesting discourses were very welcome to audiences bored by the daily routines of middle class industrial or rural life. Preaching narrative sermons was not as much a theological decision as it was a market decision. In other words, preachers were tempted to entertain or provide sensational experiences in worship. This gave rise to the "pulpit princes" who found popularity cross-denominationally.

Perhaps the most famous "pulpit prince" of the nineteenth century was Charles Grandison Finney. Finney, was strongly influenced by the Methodist tradition of revivalism and camp meeting preaching. By the same token, he influenced Methodists with his promotion of protracted meetings, social reform, encouragement of female participation, and use of the "anxious bench."[74] Finney experimented with his "new measures revivalism" in major cities, targeting poor and middle class subjects. His revival methods, serialized in his publication, the *New York Evangelist*, were compiled as *Lectures on Revivals of Religion* (1848). Finney was criticized for assuming "doubtful positions without proof" and dogmatizing "without the least diffidence."[75] Nevertheless, it was widely read by Methodists.

Essentially, his preaching style was a type of popular drama complete with extravagant set, exaggerated gestures, and commonplace illustrations. It fed on a culture seeking pulpit princes who tantalized and excited the crowd besieged with the routine of industrialized living. Finney preached using the vocabulary of the people, whether simple farmers or sophisticated lawyers. He avoided doctrinal disputes and focused on conversion.[76] The content of his sermons was based on the Calvinistic idea of total depravity, or innate moral degradation. However, his co-opting the Methodist idea of Christian perfection led his followers to move upward towards "refined respectability."[77]

Horace Bushnell was another well-known "pulpit prince." As a Calvinist, he agreed with the notion of total depravity, but tended to de-emphasize the inability of humankind to respond to God's grace. "Take any scheme of depravity you please, there is yet nothing in it to forbid the possibility that a child should be led, in his first moral act, to cleave unto what is good and right, any more than in the first of his twentieth year."[78] Furthermore, he disagreed with the tactics of revivals. He felt that conversion is not an event restricted to the individualism of revivalism. Rather, it is a process in which the Christian is nurtured in the organic connections of community.

> Any scheme of nurture that brings up children thus for revivals of religion is a virtual abuse and cruelty. And it is none the less cruel that some pious-looking pretexts are cunningly blended with it. Instead of that steady, formative, new-creating power that ought to be exerted by holiness in the house, it looks to campaigns of force that really dispense with holiness, and it results that all the best ends of Christian nurture are practically lost.[79]

Bushnell's book, *Christian Nurture*, was criticized for "imply[ing] that a man became a Christian by education rather than by the direct change of his heart by a sovereign act of God." Despite the initial controversy surrounding the book, it gained acceptance as a guide for religious education of children.[80] Bushnell's rejection of revivalism in favor of Christian nurture was clearly reflected in the type of sermons he preached. In his sermon entitled "The Gospel of the face," he decried the misguided desire for "high preaching, sturdier arguments on points of theology, better command of logical resources, more science, more fine rhetoric, more I know not what." Rather, he insisted on seeking "the divine light of souls" manifest in "genuine good living."[81]

Methodist "pulpit princes" were to be found in the many anecdotes and memoirs published by the church press. A periodical, *The Methodist Preacher*, featured sermons from popular preachers. Though it appeared in only four volumes from 1830 to 1831, it elevated the status of preachers to property of the public domain. A book followed by the same title and featured sermons on "doctrinal and practical subjects" written by such notables as Bishop Elijah Hedding, Dr. Wilbur Fisk, Dr. Nathan Bangs, and Dr. John Durbin. Wilbur Fisk, preaching in Broadway Tabernacle, New York, on the occasion of the American Bible Society, gave his famous sermon on the "transition age" with utopian vision. "The Bible – the Bible must direct and control the wheels of government, the principles of education, the character of the rising generation: this is our spiritual palladium, the glory of the churches, the honour [sic] of the nation, the salvation of the world."[82] Fisk's qualifications as a true "pulpit prince" are doubtful. In a memorial service for Fisk, Bangs lauded his oratory style as "near to perfection," but his homiletical ability was definitely too dependent on logic. "His sermons were generally of a didactic character, and on this account might have appeared to those who did not fully enter into his views, and follow his chain of reasoning, somewhat dry and dull."[83]

D. Holmes, the editor of the book, *Methodist Preacher*, lauded Bangs more for his overall actions in the church than his preaching. "Then the venerable Dr. Nathan Bangs, eminently worthy to be classed with the Apostles of American Methodism; he has by his pen, his pulpit labors, and personal influence, done more to promote the growth and prosperity of the church of his choice, than any other living man."[84] Bangs elicited his own imitators, especially students of the ministry.[85] John Durbin, lesser known of the four, was much later described as "one of the most magnetic advocates and preachers, both on the platform and in the pulpit, that the Church in America ever produced."[86]

By far the most famous Methodist "pulpit prince" was Matthew Simpson, "the peerless orator of the American pulpit."[87] Besides rising to the rank of Bishop, Simpson was celebrated nationally as a confidant of President Lincoln. He offered prayer at Lincoln's wake. He also presided over the stately burial service.

> While minute guns sounded, and a choir of 250 voices sang hymns on the State House steps. With General Hooker at its head, the long procession started towards Oak Ridge. The cemetery reached, the choir sang again while the body was placed in the tomb. A minister offered a prayer, another read scripture, a third read the second inaugural. The choir sang a dirge, and Bishop Simpson pronounced the funeral oration. There was a closing prayer, the Doxology, a benediction. Slowly, silently, the vast crowd dispersed.[88]

Late in life, Bishop Simpson was elected to deliver the prestigious Lyman Beecher Lectures on Preaching. His remarks reveal that Methodism was influenced in part by Bushnell's emphasis on Christian nurture rather than immediate conversion. Furthermore, Simpson suggested that preaching extemporaneously, so coveted by Methodists at the beginning of the century, was no longer a desirable or necessary skill.[89] Still, preachers of their era, the Gilded Age, were warned of making their sermons into heartless essays.[90]

The eventual decline of extemporaneous preaching among the less famous preachers may be attributed to the decrease in oratory skills, emphasis on academics, and intellectual demands of the congregation.[91] On the other hand, the Methodist "pulpit princes," certainly excelling in those three areas, each developed his own particular style of oratory which marked them as outstanding preachers. The downside was the popular messengers risked becoming more interesting than the message.[92] The "princes" influenced many imitators and devoted hearers who fashioned preaching palaces around the pulpit. The strength of these preachers may have influenced the revisions of the service. By the 1860s, the *Disciplines* of both the Methodist Episcopal Church and the Methodist Episcopal Church, South dropped the requirement to read a chapter each of the New and Old Testaments. Rather, preachers focused on a text or word often as a pretext for a topical sermon. The resulting message reflected the preacher's fancy more than the full sense of the scripture in context.[93] It is interesting to note that with the exception of occasional services, topical sermons before the Civil War seldom addressed the slavery issue. Rather, such preaching was relegated to the abolition, antislavery, and pro-slavery contingents.[94]

Rev. Dr. Nathan Bangs as elder statesman of American Methodism. His hands are posed on a stack of books, a tribute to his role in the Methodist Book Concern. Photo attributed to Mathew Brady.

3 SONGS OF PRAISE

Sinners through the camp are falling,

Deep distress their souls pervades,

Wondering why they are not rolling

In the dark infernal shades.[95]

J. Ernest Rattenbury said, "The greatest of all the specific religious values of
Methodism is to be found in its hymnody."[96] At least sixteen Methodist songbooks
were printed in the United States between 1805 and 1840, and one more in 1843.
These songbooks were principally compilations of songs made popular at camp
meetings and revival meetings. Perhaps the three most popular of these songbooks
included: *Hymns and Spiritual Songs*, edited by Stith Mead, 1805; *Spiritual Song Book*,
edited by David B. Mintz, 1805; and *The Pilgrim Songster*, edited by Thomas S.
Hinde, 1810.[97]

Accounts of worship at early Methodist meetings reveal an atmosphere
resplendent with emotional fervor and vigorous singing. Singing may have been
more prominent in camp meetings than in Wesley's congregations.[98] However,
quantity did not guarantee quality in the songs and hymns. The cherished hymns
of Wesley and Watts were more frequently reduced to warm up exercises for
revivalist songs. While the Wesleys attempted to add dignity to hymns as a vital

part of Christian worship, camp meeting preachers were accused of reducing the hymn to "doggerel."[99] The main objection to the camp meeting songs their tendency towards repetition and textual simplification. "Verses were shortened, refrains added, and expressions and ejaculations interpolated."[100] An example of the popular revival songs of the period is "Stop, poor sinner!"

> Stop, poor sinner! Stop and think.
>
> Before you farther go!
>
> Can you sport upon the brink
>
> Of everlasting wo [sic]?
>
> Hell beneath is gaping wide,
>
> Vengeance waits the dread command
>
> Soon he'll stop your sport and pride,
>
> And sink you with the damn'd.[101]

The four major themes of camp meeting songs were: pilgrimage; centrality of Jesus; gathered church; and personal faith assurance.[102] Although these themes resonated well with Methodism's evangelical message, they were still too shallow in terms of theological content. Nathan Bangs disliked the weak theology and judged the lyrics of camp meeting songs as inferior. It must be remembered that he was a strong advocate of Christian perfection, a prevalent theme within Wesley hymns. He testified to a personal experience of sanctification that was not dramatic, but significant in scope of meaning.

My supplications were importunate, so that I know not how

33

long I continued to pray. When I ceased, I sank down into an inexpressible calmness, as lying passive at the feet of God. I felt relieved and comforted, as though I had been 'cleansed from all filthiness of the flesh and spirit.' I had no extraordinary rapture, no more than I had often experienced before, but such a sense of my own littleness that I thought, 'What a wonder is it that God condescends to notice me at all!' All my inward distress was gone. I could look up with a childlike composure and trust, and behold God as my heavenly Father. We staid all night, and the next morning in family prayer I seemed surrounded with the divine glory. I certainly was filled at that time with the 'perfect love which casteth out fear,' for I had no fear of death or judgement.[103]

Charles Wesley considered "perfection" and "sanctification" as interchangeable terms. His use of words related to "perfection" appears almost five times more frequently than "sanctification" words, especially in his later hymns. Wesley's preference for the term "perfection" was due to poetic rather than theological considerations.[104] Bangs also used the terms "perfection" and "sanctification" interchangeably.

I care not by what name this great blessing be designated, whether holiness, sanctification, perfect love, Christian perfection, so long as is meant by it an entire consecration of soul and body to God, accompanied with faith that he accepts the sacrifice through the merits of Christ alone.[105]

Curiously, there is no exact definition of "perfection" to be found in the *corpus* of Charles Wesley's hymns. However, a journal entry dated Monday September 26, 1740 gives a revealing glimpse of his understanding of the doctrine of perfection. According to Charles Wesley, perfection is "utter dominion over sin, constant peace, and love and joy in the Holy Ghost; the full assurance of faith, righteousness, and true holiness."[106] He interpreted perfection as the sanctifying work of the Holy Spirit. There are both inward and outward elements of perfection in Wesley hymns.[107] A prime example of a Charles Wesley hymn on personal holiness is "Forth in Thy Name." It is probably the most graphic of the hymns dealing with perfection. The tone is contrition and repentance. The goal is to "sanctify the whole." Here, the idea of entire sanctification appears in the hymnody.

> Give me to bear thy easy yoke,
>
> And every moment watch and pray,
>
> And still to things eternal look,
>
> And hasten to thy glorious day.[108]

John Wesley considered Christian perfection as more as teleological, not a static condition. Christians are made free by grace "not to commit sin" so they could live in active holiness. However, "perfection" does not equivocate justification and sanctification. Albert C. Outler explained that John Wesley considered "perfection" as "correlated with the whole process of Christian maturation and hope."[109] Although Bangs was informed of John Wesley's writings on Christian perfection, his interpretation more closely resembled Charles Wesley on "sanctification."

In addition to reading the sacred Scriptures with diligence and prayer, and conversing with God's people in reference to it, I read Mr. Wesley's 'Plain Account of Christian Perfection,' some portions of Mr. Fletcher's writings on the subject, and was fully convinced of its necessity, nature, and fruits, so that I sought it understandingly, and found it, to the joy of my heart.[110]

Bangs commended sanctification in his writings as a transformative experience to be sought after for holy living. He published his definitive treatise on sanctification in 1851.[111] More importantly, his promotion of Wesleyan hymnody, as a hymnal editor, kept this theme of spirituality alive long after he lost his own national clout. Furthermore, perfectionist spirituality contributed greatly to respectability. A person moving on to perfection became more respectable in the process.[112]

Singing forms such an interesting and important branch of divine service, that every effort to improve the science of sacred music should meet with corresponding encouragement. Nothing tends more, when rightly performed, to elevate the mind, and tune it to the strains of pure devotion...Indeed, every considerable revival of true godliness has been attended, not only with the cultivation and enlargement of knowledge in general, but of sacred poetry and music in particular.[113]

In 1820 Bangs, acting as the new editor of the Book Concern, took on the task of editing a new hymn book. He hoped that reintroducing the "practical and experimental divinity" of the Wesleys would quell any unruly religious enthusiasm. Thus, the revision committee placed control on the inferior revivalist songs by returning to the sound standards of Wesley and Watts. "Watts you need not despise; but the Wesleys you will hold in the highest estimation; for, if they may not be ranked among the sublimest of poets, they are certainly among the most pious and spiritual."[114]   The new edition was considered necessary to correct the problems associated with an unauthorized *Pocket Hymn-Book* by Robert Spence of York. His unsolicited publication and distribution was not appreciated by John Wesley. At the end of the day, grace prevailed in the matter so that Wesley and Spence reconciled their relationship.

> [Spence] had published a Pocket Hymnbook in which he had
> included many of Mr. Wesley's most popular hymns. As this
> occurred just at the time Mr. Wesley was contemplating a similar
> volume, the latter in his preface reflected upon the action of the
> York bookseller in vigorous terms. The sharp passage was soon
> forgiven and forgotten, and when they next met it was in a
> friendly spirit.[115]

Spence's hymn book, though unauthorized, became very popular in Britain and America. It was so sought after that Wesley grudgingly incorporated some of it into his own hymn book, referring to the additions as "grievous doggerel."[116] Wesley was cautious not to allow this situation to overtake him again.

> Many gentlemen have done my brother and me (though without
> naming us) the honour to reprint many of our hymns. Now they
> are perfectly welcome so to do, provided they print them just as
> they are. But I desire they would not attempt to mend them--for
> really they are not able. None of them is able to mend either the
> sense or the verse. Therefore I must beg of them one of these
> two favours: either to let them stand just as they are, to take
> them for better or worse; or to add the true reading in the
> margin, or at the bottom of the page, that we may no longer be
> accountable either for the nonsense or for the doggerel of other

men.[117]

Even with the availability of Wesley's 1780 hymn book, Spence's *Pocket Hymn-Book* was published and distributed in America as early as 1786.[118] Bangs was concerned that the *Pocket Hymn-Book* was too small and lacked the necessary content for private devotion or public worship. Therefore, an enlarged edition was published in 1808, but it still contained very few Wesley hymns and corrupted and incomplete lyrics.[119] Interest in producing an authorized tune book resulted in the publication of *David's Companion* in 1808. It clearly reflected the music popular at historic John Street Church. Although it was approved in principle by the General Conference of 1808, revised in 1810 and again in 1817, it never gained official approval.[120]

The New York Annual Conference commissioned a revision of the hymnbook in 1819 with the intent of presenting it to the following General Conference. The preface included a note of explanation for the revision which restored the glory of Wesleyan hymnody to the song book.

> The greater part of the hymns contained in the former edition are retained in this, and several from Wesley and Coke's collections, not before published in this country, as added. The principal improvements which have been made consist in restoring those which had been altered, as is believed, for the worse, to their original state, as they came from the poetical pen of the Wesleys; for the following hymns were, except a few which have been taken from other authors, composed by the Rev. John and Charles Wesley--names that will ever be held dear and in high estimation by every lover of sacred poetry.[121]

The success of the 1821 hymn book seemed guaranteed by the tremendous growth of the market. This fact did not escape the notice of certain opponents to the Methodist movement. The *Quarterly Christian Spectator* severely criticized the Book Concern for placing such a high centrality on the Methodist hymn book. Worse yet, they accused them of taking financial advantage of their constituents.

> Every Methodist, rich or poor, must have a hymn book: and multitudes who attend on the worship of that denomination without adding themselves to the 420, 000, must have hymn books also. All these books are published at one office from stereotype plates, and are sold at nearly or quite double the price at which a bookseller might publish them and realize a profit, besides paying for the use of copy-right.[122]

The charge that only one set of plates was used in the printing is entirely false. A second set of plates was made to lower the production cost of the new hymnal. Evidence for this is in a letter (1821) sent to Martin Ruter at the Book Concern's Cincinnati publishing house.

> We have commenced stereotyping the New Hymn Book, and shall have a set of plates made also for your use, as by having two sets made at the same time they come much lower. But we shall not use them until the present Edition is out.[123]

Bangs answered his critics in a series of articles published in the *Christian Advocate and Journal* and *Zion's Herald*. By unanimous vote of the New York

Conference, the articles were compiled into a pamphlet and distributed as the *Reviewer Answered.* The articles defended the publishing practices of the Methodist Book Concern against the criticisms of Congregationalist "officers in Yale College" who "vented their spleen" against them.[124] Thus, in the midst of external criticism, Bangs was able to retain control over controversies surrounding the production of hymn books. Furthermore, a defense of the publication rights suggests a struggle to maintain order in publishing and distribution. The preface of the 1836 hymnbook included a disclaimer and a solemn warning, bolstered by an episcopal *imprimatur*, against purchasing unauthorized versions.

> We are the more delighted with this design, as no personal advantage is concerned, but the public good alone. For after the necessary expenses of publications are discharged, we shall make it a noble charity, by applying the profits arising therefrom to religious and charitable purposes.
>
> No motive of a sinister nature has therefore influenced us in any degree to publish this excellent compilation. As the profits of the former editions have been scrupulously applied as above, so the same appropriation of the profits of the present shall be conscientiously observed. We must therefore earnestly entreat you, if you have any respect for the authority of the conference, or of us, or any regard for the prosperity of the Church of which you are members and friends, to purchase no Hymnbooks but what are published by our own agents, and signed with the names of your bishops. And as we intend to keep a constant supply, the complaint of our congregations, "that they cannot procure our Hymnbooks," will be stopped.[125]

Sandwiched between the preface and the first hymn is an intriguing repetition of the warning against purchasing unauthorized hymnbooks. This double warning was perhaps the most brazen exercise of bureaucratic authority ever witnessed in the MEC.

CAUTION

All persons desirous of possessing the true revised and improved official edition of the Methodist Hymnbook, with the Supplement, are advised to be careful to examine the *imprint*, and to purchase those only published by our General Book Agents, for the Methodist Episcopal Church, or by the Agents at Cincinnati.[126]

An unfortunate fired destroyed the Methodist Book Concern in New York along with the printing plates for the 1821 hymnbook, 1832 revision. Bangs issued the 1836 *Hymnal* along with a supplement of ninety hymns.[127]

As the plates for the Hymn-book were destroyed by that disastrous event, by which it has become necessary to prepare a new set, we have availed ourselves of this opportunity to add the following Supplement, consisting chiefly of hymns adapted to special occasions, such as dedications, anniversaries, &c. Some of these are original, having been prepared expressly for this purpose, but the most of them are selected from the festival and other Hymns of the late Rev. Charles Wesley, than whom no man ever united the spirit of poetry, fervent piety, and evangelical sentiment more firmly and delightfully together.[128]

Bangs was keen to recover the theological richness of Wesley hymns for Methodist worship. It is significant in that, even with the supplement, it did not contain works by an American author nor did it acknowledge camp meeting songs.[129] By issuing the 1836 edition, Bangs re-emphasized the importance of understanding the Methodist hymn book as "a little body of experimental and practical divinity."[130]

Furthermore, the re-inclusion of Wesley hymns revived an important source of theological documents.[131]

An intriguing restatement of the role of hymnody in worship appeared in the preface of the 1836 and 1843 hymn books. It defined and limited the sphere of private and public worship. Thus, the controls were extended to dimensions heretofore unspecified.

> In presenting this revised Hymnbook to you for your use, we humbly trust that we are putting into your hands one of the choicest selections of evangelical hymns, suitable for private devotion, as well as for family, social, and public worship, by which you will be much aided in the performance of these important parts of divine service.[132]

The 1836 revised hymn book provided American Methodists a more faithful and complete text of Wesley hymns. This was improved by the 1849 revision which was touted as "the fullest and most correct presentation of Wesleyan poetry" with works by American authors.[133]

The value of the hymns books for personal spirituality was well recognized. Nathan Bangs noted that he used the hymn book to share devotions with his spiritual father, Joseph Sawyer. "At the breakfast table on Sunday morning each of the company repeated a passage from the Holy Scriptures, after which, at Dr. Bangs' instance, they cited each a stanza from the Church Hymn Book."[134] After reciting a stanza from John Wesley's translation of Gerhardt's "Jesu, Thy boundless love to me," Bangs was overwhelmed with emotion and "could utter but a word or two."[135]

The editing and distribution of authorized hymn books guaranteed the promotion of the enlarged authority of the MEC, but did not guarantee obedience to it. Thus, resistance against denominational control and formalism continued in the face of efforts to maintain Methodist respectability.

> Improvements doubtless may be made: yet, as a whole, for our congregational singing, we question whether a better guide can be found that the 'Methodist Harmonist'... We beg leave, in closing, to express our gratification that the compilers of our Tunebook concur with us in deprecating the frequent introduction into ordinary congregational singing of fugue tunes, and a complicated artificial harmony. We have often felt and mourned over this as a lamentable destroyer of the glory of *Methodist* congregational singing; and as the chief, if not the sole cause, in fact, of that deplorable evil so extensively, we fear, creeping in among us, by which this heavenly part of worship is confined, as in the orchestras of public shows or theatres, to a few individuals, technically styled *the singers*.[136]

Bishop John Emory was a great supporter of the hymns of the Wesleys and Watts. Thus he supported the revision of the hymn book directed by Nathan Bangs. The revised hymn book brought a welcome sense of order to singing. At the same time congregational singing was de-emphasized in favor of choirs. The General Conference of 1832 authorized a reprinting of the 1822 *Methodist Harmonist* improved by the inclusion of anthems, sentences, and pieces. Karen B. Westerfield Tucker suggests that this may indicate acceptance of the new forms at the very least on the official level.[137] Emory preferred congregational singing to bad harmonies or "singers." When the *Harmonist* (c. 1837) was published as a supplement to the

Methodist Hymnbook, Emory offered this commentary on the value of congregational singing. On the other hand, Emory was cautious about corrupting congregational singing with poor lyrics, harmonies, or instrumental music. Citing Dr. Adam Clarke, he warned:

> *Melody*, which is allowed to be the most proper for devotional music, is now sacrificed to an exuberant *harmony*, which requires not only many *different kinds of voices*, but *different musical instruments*, to support it. And by these preposterous means, the *simplicity* of the Christian worship is destroyed, and all edification totally prevented.[138]

The Wesleyan predilection for congregational singing notwithstanding, American as well as British Methodists were eager to enhance their worship experience with improved music. The original disciplinary instruction for public worship suggested that the preacher, rather a "singer," give out the words of a hymn.[139] The improvements of music eventually removed the preacher from this role. The *Discipline 1856* advised that song leaders be chosen for the congregation and that "due attention be given to the cultivation of sacred music."[140]

Union Theological Seminary in New York took the lead in cultivating sacred music as a discipline. Presbyterians had long relied on "precentors" to give the pitch and lead the tunes. The trouble was that middle class constituents, now quite familiar with stage performances and concert hall music, were not easily pacified by dull or substandard music.[141] In 1837, six months after the establishment of the school, Abner Jones was elected as Professor of Sacred Music. Several other notable figures followed in his footsteps. Students at Union formed the Haydn Society for the revival and study of classical sacred music. The Society remained active from 1841 to 1852. During this time composers Thomas Hastings and Lowell Mason energized and elevated the music of New York churches. In 1852, George Frederick Root took the baton at the seminary. He pooled his fame by collaborating with Chauncey Marvin Cady and Fanny Crosby. In 1855, Root convinced the Chancellor of New York University to confer the first Doctor of Music degree on veteran composer and music educator Lowell Mason. Under Mason's term, auditors were permitted to attend lectures on music.[142] Throughout this entire period, instruction in sacred music was widely disseminated amongst New York composers, choirs, organists, and pianists.[143]

Further evidence that congregational singing diminished in importance is in the change in the rules for singing in worship. In order to avoid formality, it was suggested that the [congregational] singing be limited. "By not singing too much at once; seldom more than five or six verses."[144] The *Discipline 1856* amended this rule by reducing the number of suggested verses to four or five.[145]

> The primitive Methodist preachers knew well how to accommodate themselves to the habits, as also to the fare of [settlers]....The early memoranda before me afford not a few glimpses of this primitive life of the frontier – crowded congregations in log-huts or barns – some of the hearers seated, some standing, some filling the unglazed casements, some thronging the overhanging trees – startling interjections thrown into the sermon by eccentric listeners – violent polemics between the preacher and headstrong sectarists, the whole assembly sometimes involved in the earnest debate, some for, some against him, and ending in general confusion. A lively Methodist hymn was usually the best means of restoring order in such cases.[146]

Many Methodists prized the enthusiastic experiences associated with camp meeting religion. Therefore, they attempted to extend the revivalistic worship experience into the venue of established congregations. In some cases, as evidenced above, hymn singing could restore order to an unwieldy crowd. However, order came only by the enforcement of strict discipline. This must have been a consideration when Wesley's "Rules for Congregational Singing" were reprinted in *The Methodist Magazine*.[147]

Although Nathan Bangs appreciated a genuine heart-felt worship, he did not tolerate disorder. As a pastor, he was horrified to observe excesses of demonstrative worship in the historic John Street Church in Manhattan. Bangs testified that he "witnessed...a spirit of pride, presumption, and bigotry, impatience of scriptural restraint and moderation, clapping of the hands, screaming, and even jumping, which marred and disgraced the work of God."[148] He quickly laid down the law to his parishioners, basing his action on a dream in which he slew the "snake" of disorder with the "whip" of the *Methodist Discipline*. One disgruntled congregant bemoaned Bangs' insistence on decorum. "Mr. Bangs had done more injury that evening to the cause of God than the could ever be able to make amends for."[149]

The importance of the *Discipline* in maintaining order in worship cannot be understated. Although the *Discipline* was published following the Christmas Conference of 1784, it did not at that time regulate the form of service. Such was passed on from preacher to preacher. Unquestionably, the *Discipline* surpassed Wesley's *Sunday Service* in this particular role in the critical year after Wesley's death in 1791. The *Sunday Service* was abandoned and the "sacramental services" entered the pages of the *Discipline*.[150] Seeing the need for a formal book of worship, the General Conference of 1820 appointed Joshua Soule, Nathan Bangs, and Daniel Ostrander to assist the episcopacy to revise the *Discipline*.[151] The resulting *Doctrines and Discipline, 1824* had some of the most sweeping changes to church order in the denomination's history. It outlined a formal order of worship with the addition of the Lord's Prayer enjoined for all occasions.   Methodist preachers were admonished to use this form "invariably" to avoid the temptation for free form of worship.

> In administering the ordinances, and in the burial of the dead, let the form of discipline invariably be used. Let the Lord's Prayer also be used on all occasions of public worship in concluding the first prayer, and the apostolic benediction in dismissing the congregation.[152]

The *Discipline* of 1828 also tried to enforce "uniformity" in worship. James F. White posits that the frequent language that the "ritual invariably be used" is "good evidence that it was not."[153]

The difficulty, again, was enforcing new formal modes of worship. In preparation for a General Conference in Baltimore, Bangs visited some local churches, including an African American congregation. What he saw would stay with him for the remainder of his clergy career.

> I was particularly interested in the worship of the negroes, which I here witnessed for the first time. These poor people seemed ecstatic in their gratitude for the Gospel and their hope of a better life. They shouted and 'leaped for joy;' they heard the word with intense eagerness, and their prayers and singing were

full of animation.[154]

It is not surprising that Bangs had such little contact with African Americans, considering his location in Canada and New York. He was not overtly racist, however he did consider white people superior to people of color.[155] This did not prevent him for supporting the election of Francis Burns, a black man, to become the first Missionary Bishop to Liberia.[156] It appears that Bangs was genuinely sympathetic to the social condition of African American people.

Worship styles of African American Methodists, both slave and free, reflected their particular strata of wealth and education. Slave religion was both otherworldly and worldly. That is, Christianity offered hope in deliverance for slaves who saw themselves as a type of the biblical Israel.[157] This combination of otherworldly and worldly religion is especially evident in this account of a Wesleyan watchnight service for emancipation in the British held Antigua in the West Indies in 1834.

> All was animation and eagerness. A mighty chorus of voices swelled the song of expectation and joy; and as they united in prayer, the voice of the leader was drowned in the universal acclamation of thanksgiving, and praise, and blessing, and honor, and glory, to God, who had come down for their deliverance....
>
> At the instruction of the White missionary, they went to their knees in silence as the clock tolled twelve. Then, the celebration resumed in a greater measure than before. Shouts of "Glory!" and "Alleluia!" filled the room as the now free Africans clapped, hugged, laughed, and cried. When the excitement subsided, the missionaries exercised their control by "exhorting the free people to be industrious, steady, obedient to the laws, and to show themselves in all things worthy of the high boon which God had conferred upon them."[158]

Another incident involving indecorous worship occurred in Ithaca in upstate New York. Methodists in Ithaca decided to hold their own prayer meeting, keeping their "colored" members close at hand and away from a camp meeting. "If the Methodists from the country become disorderly, we will not suffer, as the public can see the difference between the Ithaca Methodists, and the ranting Methodists from the country."[159] Thus, it is evident that Bangs was not alone in his effort to discipline Methodist worship.

As respectability became the desired image in the MEC, tighter controls were placed on order of worship. The results proved that church order was an effective means of establishing the MEC as a respectable denomination. The early successes of camp meeting and revival worship guaranteed continuance as a denominational institution. But this did not guarantee the continuance of the associated frenzied worship style. The Gilded Age witnessed the "toning down" of emotionalism and reduction of camp meetings into Chautauqua meetings.[160] The criticism of excesses were replaced by criticisms of commercialism.[161] Another faction followed in the tradition of Phoebe Palmer and John Inskip and formed camp meeting associations where they could combine holiness of body and mind.[162] Demands for regularity and order gave way to their replacement by quarterly meetings. In turn, the quarterly meeting worship diminished in enthusiasm until it became little more than miniature versions of annual conferences where reports dominated the floor. Religious fervor in the MEC cooled down and constituents adjusted to a more settled lifestyle. Preaching and singing were formalized. The Methodist penchant for spontaneity remained as a dormant sub current until it later emerged in Holiness and Pentecostal worship.

At the end of the day, Bangs considered the resulting formal mode of MEC worship closer to the original church of Christ than other denominations. "It is to be hoped that Methodists will cleave to their standards, maintain their spirituality, and be more solicitous for the inward purity and internal energy of their church, than they are for those outward decorations which may commend it to the approbation of the mere men of the world."[163] This statement reveals the ongoing tension between Bangs' desire to promote the lively evangelical religion and the quest for denominational respectability. These divergent streams of spiritual fervor and material respectability nurtured the rise of pulpit princes and formal church music. The simple Methodist chapel was no longer adequate for new forms of worship. As the next chapter will demonstrate, preaching palaces came into vogue as the sacred space of choice for respectable Methodists.

Rev. Dr. Nathan Bangs, Presidential portrait at Wesleyan University, Middletown, Connecticut.

4 METHODIST TEMPLES

Brother Taylor, you need not think that any of us Western men
are anxious about preaching to you in Boston; your way of
worship here is so different from ours in the West, that we are
confused. There's your old wooden god, the organ, bellowing
up in the gallery, and a few dandified singers lead in singing, and
really do it all. The congregation won't sing, and when you pray,
they sit down instead of kneeling. We don't worship God in the
West by proxy, or substitution. You need not give yourself any
trouble about getting a Western man to preach in your church;
we don't want to do it....[164]

The arrangement and use of sacred space of urbane Methodists in the

mid-nineteenth century changed so much that the new form was almost

unrecognizable to pioneer veterans such as Peter Cartwright. The place of the

rustic log chapels and austere wooden meeting houses was supplanted by tall

steepled stone and brick buildings with stain glass windows. Congregational

singing became less important than the sacred music led by song leaders, choirs,

and organs. Cushioned slip pews replaced the crude bench seating. Prayer was

conducted by a solitary leader while the congregation sat rather than kneel. To the

observer fresh from beyond the Appalachians, worship was more akin to a day at

the theater than church. These "evils" smacked of formality to traditionalists.

Thus, they were denounced as engendering pride and destroying spirituality. "It

gives precedence to the rich, proud, and fashionable part of our hearers, and

unavoidably blocks up the way of the poor; and no stumbling-block should be put in the way of one of these little ones that believe in Christ."[165] John Bangs denounced steeples and the inclusion of musical instruments in the church as "superfluity and needless expense."[166]

The subject of architecture, of little concern in the early lean years, became an important issue for upwardly mobile Methodists. This was especially true for those situated in proximity to the more affluent Unitarians, Episcopalians, Congregationalists, Presbyterians, and even Roman Catholics.[167] The interiors were expanded and remodeled to match the more ostentatious exteriors. The pulpit and organ split the congregation's focus during worship in two. By the early 1850s, as Cartwright found in Boston pulpits, congregations expected to be entertained by narrative preaching. Thus, they would no longer tolerate boring didactic sermons. Even in Bangs' day, the so-called "Pulpit Princes" were attracting crowds who preferred riveting narratives to dry doctrinal treatises. Galleries were built for the organs, singers, and seating. They were also used to segregate from the congregation those of lesser means and other races. This chapter will briefly discuss the how the quest for refined sacred space effected architecture, seating, and musical instruments.

> Those who have been acquainted with our circuits and stations for twenty, thirty, and forty years past, and who can compare our houses of worship then with what they are now, will be struck with the contrast, and will praise God for the improvement in this respect. In former days, most of the preaching places, more particularly in the country villages and settlements, were private houses, schoolhouses, barns, and groves; even when a church edifice was erected, a site was generally selected in some obscure retreat, remote from the centre [sic] of population, as though the Methodists were ashamed to be seen and heard by their

neighbours [sic]; and even this small edifice was frequently but half finished, and left to fall down under its own rottenness. In this respect, there is a mighty improvement, such an improvement as must be encouraging to the hearts of all God's people. Now there are large and commodious houses of worship, not only in our populous cities – where indeed many have been recently built or enlarged, and their number increased with the advancing population, – but in almost every village and considerable settlement throughout the country are found temples finished in a neat, plain style, in which the pure word of God is preached, and his ordinances duly administered.[168]

The long standing admonition that preaching chapels should be "built plain and decent"[169] no longer met the needs of the MEC. Increased prosperity naturally led to the construction of exquisite churches. Furthermore, the burgeoning growth of the Methodist movement also created a demand for more churches with larger space. American cities buckled under the population explosion fueled by the lure of industry and settlement of new immigrants. For example, in 1838 the Methodist Episcopal Church in Lowell, Massachusetts found it necessary to divide in two congregations. Chapel Hill and Wesley Chapel were created to accommodate the influx of mill workers who either came to Lowell as Methodists or converted soon after. Wesley Chapel enjoyed the growth spurt. When it was rebuilt as St. Paul's (1839), it was considered the largest MEC sanctuary in New England.[170]

By 1857, there were approximately eight thousand members and twenty-eight Methodist churches in New York City. Twenty-three of these churches were built between 1831 and 1854.[171] Money for construction was in good supply between 1831 and 1839 due to a rise in cotton prices and commodities.[172]

Bangs stated that a stationed ministry must be established to keep the converts from going to competing sects. This necessitated construction of new chapels and parsonages. For Bangs, new construction met a serious missional need in the MEC.

> You might as well go home and go to sleep, so far as Methodism is concerned, as to preach in the manner you do; for though your labors may be blessed, other sects will reap their results, and thus, so far as our own Church is concerned, you lose the fruit of your toils and sufferings....We must...go to work and build churches in all the cities and populous villages, and have preachers stationed in them, that they may perform the duties of pastors, watching over the flock and building them up in holiness.[173]

Indeed, Bangs both supported the construction of new churches and the reconfiguration of existing churches. At the very least, Bangs was noticeably present in the construction of several prominent New York churches. In 1817, Manhattan's historic John Street Methodist Church underwent a building scheme while he served as their appointed pastor. Seven years earlier Bishop Asbury suggested that: "This house must come down and something larger and better occupy its place."[174] Bangs organized and brought forward that vision for an improved building. Additional land was purchased and the original building was razed. The new building exterior was in the style of Greek Revival, the typical fashion of the period.[175] The interior retained the plainness expected of a "meeting house." Bangs preached the morning dedication sermon recounting the brief history of Methodism in America that led to the reconstruction of John Street Church.

> Notwithstanding God had so enlarged our borders, that six additional houses of worship had been erected, (including two for the people of colour[sic]), it was found that this, which is now rebuilt, was not sufficiently large to accomodate [sic] all who wished to convene for the worship of God in this place. For some time previous to the actual commencement of the work, it had been in contemplation. Having formed the resolution, you commenced on the 13th day of May last to demolish the former house. On the 22nd day of May, the foundation sermon was preached for this. Through the protection and smiles of our God, you have succeeded according to your wishes in completing a neat, elegant, and commodious house for divine worship, which we have now dedicated to the special service of Almighty God.[176]

Joshua Soule preached the evening dedication sermon. Whereas Bangs was more interested in history and statistics, Soule focused on the "object and nature of spiritual worship." This was perhaps an indication of an underlying hope for a more refined worship devoid of enthusiasm and superstition in the newly erected building.

> For want of such knowledge, enthusiasm and superstition have too often usurped the seats of Christian moderation and charity. It is not the least affliction which the church has suffered, that many of her professed friends have substituted the impulses of their passions, or the strength of their prejudices for the unerring testimony of the oracles of God; and through an indiscreet zeal have broken down those sacred barriers which the gospel has erected to guard her rights.[177]

Soule's emphasis on a proper mode of worship was a point not missed by Thomas O. Summers who reprinted it years as early as 1855 for the MEC, South under the title *Object and Nature of Religious Worship.*[178] Rebuilding John Street Church created no small discord among the congregants. The location had become more commercial than residential. "Downtown" and "uptown" members, long-time opposing church factions, argued whether the new building should be "an improvement on the architectural style of the old one."[179] The preacher in charge, Daniel Ostrander, opposed the reconstruction plan, apparently in retaliation for not being invited to preach the dedication sermon. Despite this unfortunate episode, the church was rebuilt and even served as "a model for many later structures in the country."[180] The importance of John Street Church was elevated to a higher level, serving its most critical leadership role in the local community and the MEC nationally after the reconstruction.[181]

In several MECs proper preaching palaces were appointed with exquisite furnishings such as carved wooden pulpits, altar rails, and communion tables. Tall pulpits were also lowered to reduced the awkwardness of climbing steps.[182] The impression given was that of formality and solemnity. Even at John Street Church, largely unchanged on the outside, the atmosphere of opulence prevailed inside and out.

> Arriving at John-street, the corpse was taken into the Methodist church, which was filled to overflowing; an eloquent and impressive discourse was delivered by the Rev. T. Birch; and the service concluded by a solemn and affecting prayer from the Rev. Henry Chase. The procession was then again formed, and proceeded to the steamboat ferry; where it crossed over to Brooklyn, Long-Island: here the corpse was again taken into the

Methodist church, when the Rev. Nathan Bangs read the 15th chapter of 1 Corinthians, and concluded by reading the burial service, after which the body was silently committed to the grave. His voice, while living, had often been heard in this temple, and there "his body, precious even in death, sleeps near the spot where the doctrines of the Christian denomination to which he was attached were first preached in America: – there, it will await that morning of which he loved, when living, to speak, and of which he sometimes spoke in entrancing language – the morning of the resurrection."[183]

The 1825 funeral service for Rev. John Summerfield illustrates the link between formality of ritual and architecture. It is also significant that an inscribed black and white marble cenotaph was placed in John Street Church as a tribute to the deceased. It is described as "finely polished" and "elegantly sculptured."[184] The practice of installing cenotaphs was later abandoned. In time, memorials were given in the form of financial gifts and endowments. Increased cash flow from memorials enabled churches to upgrade their furnishings to suit the more refined tastes of congregants.

The general move from plain chapels to exquisite churches began about 1820. In the early days, the simple Methodist chapels served farmers, day laborers, and mechanics. The new stately churches were built to accommodate the tastes of Methodist lawyers, physicians, politicians, and merchants.[185] Yet, some stubbornly continued the Methodist tradition of building "plain and decent" houses of worship as a protest against the appetite for formality in the class of upwardly mobile Methodists.[186]

As the church became more middle class, so the desire increased for keeping up appearances. In 1835, Second Wesleyan Chapel in New York was built in the same design as First Wesleyan Chapel on Vestry Street. Nathan Bangs preached the morning dedicatory sermon. The building boasted seating for nine hundred, carpeting, cushions, and a custom mahogany pulpit. In 1856, Second Wesleyan Chapel accepted an offer to sell their property to St. Philip's Protestant Episcopal Church. The chapel was sold and moved to Fourth Avenue and Twenty-second Street, the site of the old wooded chapel known as Calvary Protestant Episcopal Church. The new church was now known as St. Paul's Methodist Episcopal Church. Nathan Bangs laid the cornerstone for a more ambitious building.[187] When completed, St. Paul's MEC was judged as surpassing the glories of Second Wesleyan Chapel.

> Although some persons aim most at intellectual purity and simplification, for others *richness* is the supreme imaginative requirement. When one's mind is strongly of this type, as individual religion will hardly serve the purpose. The inner need is rather of something institutional and complex, majestic in the hierarchic interrelatedness of its parts, with authority descending from stage to stage, and at every stage objects for adjectives of mystery and splendor, derived in the last resort from the Godhead who is the fountain and culmination of the system. One feels then as if in presence of some vast incrusted work of jewelry or architecture; one hears the multitudinous liturgical appeal; one gets the honorific vibration coming from every quarter. [188]

William James' definition of sacred space is descriptive of what became of the character of Methodists who were estranged from the faith of their pioneer fathers and mothers. Having moved up in social strata above the crises of the poor, they found more grace in aesthetics than in individual experiences. Thus, they were open to changes in fashion and architecture which were the domain of the refined elite.

Archaeological discoveries in the ancient Mediterranean cities of Herculaneum and Pompeii influenced European designers to create classical Greek motifs. The Greek revival in England was inspired by Stuart and Revett's *Antiquities of Athens*, (ca.1762). But it was the architect Benjamin Henry Latrobe who introduced the Ionic design of Philadelphia's Bank of Pennsylvania.[189] Greek styles were also imported to America in the form of fashion design books and furniture and art reproductions. Therefore, many of the rebuilt and new churches of the years between 1820 and 1850 were in the Greek Revival style complete with Doric columns and pediments suggestive of classical Greece.[190]

In response to an undercurrent of Anglo-Catholic thought, British architects and theorists rejected the pagan-based Greek style and began a series of discussions about the superior Christian attributes of pointed, or Gothic, architecture. In *The True Principles of Pointed or Christian Architecture*, (1841), Augustus W. Pugin, argued that Gothic was the true Christian form. However, Pugin was suspect because of his conversion to Roman Catholicism.[191] Critics were concerned that embracing Pugin's principles was tantamount to deferring to Edward Pusey's scandalous inclinations to reunite with Rome. At length, theorists were able to separate Puseyism from Gothic architecture. At the same time, a renewal of high church liturgy was being promoted in the Anglican Church by John

Henry Newman and the Oxford movement. This complex network of theorists and movements has been referred to *in toto* as the "Tractarian-Oxford-Anglo-Catholic-Ritualistic movement."[192] Architects, theorists, and liturgist agreed that Gothic was the legitimate historical heritage of the Anglican Church.[193]

It is unclear how the Gothic Revival entered the mainstream of Methodist thought. However, it is certain that the Gothic, or ecclesiological, movement made its way to America by way of publications and increased international exchanges with Britain. Ecclesiological societies sprang up promoting the renaissance of Gothic architecture. The Cambridge Camden Society was formed in 1839 by students J. M. Neale and Benjamin Webb and their tutor Rev. T. Thorpe to "promote the study of Ecclesiastical architecture and the restoration of mutilated architectural remains." The society produced several pamphlets including: *Hints for the Practical Study of Ecclesiastical Antiquities* (1839); *Church Enlargement and Church Arrangement* (1842); *Twenty-three Reasons for Getting Rid of Church Pues*; and *Hints to Workmen Engaged in Churches.*[194] By mid-century the Ecclesiological Society had become sufficiently powerful to intimidate architects into building Gothic style buildings.[195]

In America, one of the most influential publications on Gothic architecture was Bishop John Henry Hopkins' *An Essay on Gothic Architecture*, (1836). It was the first such book published in the United States.[196] Hopkins, and other thinkers sympathetic to the Oxford Movement, suggested a return to Gothic architecture as the true Christian form of the art. John Summerson has suggested that the movement "represents a surgence of that hard bourgeois Puritanism half-hidden in the 18th century which had never expressed itself emotionally but at last seized the opportunity to do so" in literature and architecture.[197] Whatever the reasons, the idea made a great impression on Bishop William Rollinson Whittingham, Protestant Episcopal Bishop of Maryland, who began promoting construction of parish churches with deep chancels and half-Georgian, half-Gothic style.[198]

Most notable of the American neo-Gothic edifices was Trinity [Protestant Episcopal] Church, located in New York City only a few blocks from John Street Methodist Episcopal Church. Richard Upjohn, a British architect influenced by Pugin's designs, began building Trinity Church in 1839 and completed it in 1846. His first buildings were in the Greek Revival style. He was influenced towards Gothic architecture by the writings of famed British architects Pugin and Britton. Reverend Jonathan Mayhew Wainwright, a high ranking Protestant Episcopal cleric, also guided Upjohn in thinking in terms of High Church Anglicanism.[199]

The lavish Gothic design of Trinity Church epitomized the Anglican desire for returning to authentic "Catholic" architecture. "Its sanctuary was paved with coloured [sic] marble, and contained an altar of panelled oak, backed by an elaborate oak reredos, the panels of which were painted with the Lord's Prayer, the Creed and the Ten Commandments."[200] It was fashioned in eighteenth century English Perpendicular Gothic. By contrast, James Renwick built New York City's St. Patrick's Roman Catholic Cathedral in French Gothic style.[201]

One reason why low church Protestants were attracted to the Gothic Revival in architecture may have been a growing appetite for refinement, education, and taste. The Gothic form was appealing because it was not sectarian, but "simply Christian."[202] It is significant that up to the Civil War, American Protestants often purchased a set of architectural plans and contracted a builder rather than hire an architect.[203] In Ottawa, Canadian Methodists were advised to consult with architects. They concluded that Gothic architecture was necessary to insure survival of the Methodists in their upwardly mobile community.[204] The downside of the Gothic plan was the long chancel hindered the hearing of the preacher by the congregation. This did not go without notice to Methodists who preferred to hear the sermon. The following except from the *Christian Advocate* is anything but irenic.

> Most of our readers have never had the inconvenience of worshipping in a church in which they could not hear the preacher...It is so outrageous that it can be called doing nothing less than the work of the devil. In the very place where, of all others, God's kingdom is to be enlarged and Satan's power overthrown, there to be occupied in speaking to the air! It does seem as if the devil was engaged in the structure of many of our church buildings. One of the best contributions to the spread of the gospel would be, to tear down every such structure, and then to take good care that the architect of the new building was not possessed of a demon, that he should do the same folly over. Then let him build a church in which all can see, all hear, and all be comfortable.[205]

Bishop Matthew Simpson, enthused by the growing wealth of Methodists, encouraged the construction of Christ Church, Pittsburgh which began in 1853 and was completed in 1855. Simpson described it as "a beautiful edifice, and the first church of more modern architecture built by the Methodists in America."[206]

Indeed, it was the first Gothic Revival Methodist church in America.[207] The MEC's experiments with Gothic were not widespread. By the time the MEC entered the Gilded Age, the Romanesque styling and theater inspired floor plans became the preferred form of architecture.[208] Although the MEC architecture took a different direction, the Romanesque, the construction of Gothic churches in proximity of their churches both provoked and inspired better architecture for public worship.

In 1832, Lewis Tappan, Charles Grandison Finney's chief financier, leased the opulent Chatham Theatre in New York for its excellent acoustics and stage presence. He refitted the auditorium with an enlarged pulpit and large windows. Otherwise, it retained much of the character of the original theater space.[209] The auditorium had three tiers of galleries with adjoining rooms for prayer meetings and lectures. The success of this first preaching palace was quickly realized. In spite of a devastating cholera epidemic, which also infected Finney, the Second Free Presbyterian Church, or Chatham Street Chapel, fostered seven new churches. Although rich patrons paid most of the bills, their converts consisted mostly of middle class and lower class. According to Finney, "This was what we aimed to accomplish, to preach the Gospel especially to the poor."[210] In only two years, against the objections of his architect, Finney himself designed the first purpose built preaching palace known as Broadway Tabernacle.[211] Revival meetings had a nice benefit for New York Methodists. A protracted revival at Allen Street Church, MEC, resulted in the erection of seven new and two rebuilt churches.[212]

The earlier protests against the Gothic renewal may have slowed down updating plain chapels into exquisite churches. However, it did not prevent others from zealously pressing forward in the construction of Methodist preaching palaces. Methodists living in Washington, D.C., had lamented the palpable absence of any notable Methodist architecture of respectable worth in the Capitol. In response, they formed a committee to study the possibility of constructing a proper memorial to American Methodism. The report was delivered to the General Conference of 1852 to address what they considered a national problem.

> Every one who feels a just and jealous concern for the respectability and success of our fondly–cherished Methodism, must see and regret the same deficiency, and desire to supply it by every justifiable means at his disposal...
>
> *Resolved*, 1st , That we cordially approve of the erection of a new house of worship for the Methodist Episcopal Church in the city of Washington, as contemplated by our brethren in their memorial.
>
> *Resolved*, 2nd, That, regarding the success of this enterprise as of high importance to the interests of Methodism throughout the country, we will give it our individual influence in our respective annual conferences, and by all appropriate means aid in its promotion.[213]

The construction plan for the national church was approved at the General Conference in 1852. This was the last General Conference which Bangs sat as a delegate, though he was not a member of the memorial committee. Nevertheless, the acceptance of this proposal embodied Bangs' fifty year travail for respectability.[214] Frank M. Bristol, a contemporary Methodist preacher, noted that the "National Church of Methodism" was a special project of Bishop Matthew Simpson. "From the foundation stone, laid before the Civil War, to its completion and final redemption from all debt, the great Bishop took a pride and interest in it as the child of his brain."[215] It is clear that Bishop Simpson took up the cause for respectability from this time forward. He preached the dedication sermon on October 23, 1854. When Metropolitan Memorial Church was completed in 1869, it was strikingly different from nearby Lovely Lane Chapel. The new church boasted a 220 foot spire and towering members such as President Ulysses S. Grant who once served as chair of the trustees. It was the ultimate monument to respectable Methodism in America.

> It was determined to build a new house, which by persevering exertion was effected; the new house was completed and dedicated in the spring of 1822. It is built of brick, on the northwest corner of the public square, or green, 68 by 80 feet, and has a basement story of about 67 feet square. It is plain and convenient, and reflects much honour [sic] upon the builders. The only objection that can be made to it is, the slips have doors, and part of them are either sold, with the privilege of redeeming them after ten years, or rented – but the whole of the gallery is free, and both sides of the lower part, with exception of one or two seats. This by many is thought a very great convenience, as they can have their families sit together.[216]

Changes in social mores stretched the boundaries of male/female relationships, even in church seating. The historic MEC rules did not permit the sexes to sit together in chapels. "Q. Is there any Exception to the Rule 'Let the Men and Women sit apart.' A. There is no Exception. Let them sit apart in all our Chapels."[217] Actually, Wesley did provide for an exception in certain cases. "In those galleries where they have always sat together, they may do so still. But let them sit apart everywhere below, an in all new-erected galleries."[218] Methodist chapels were arranged so that men and women entered in separate entrances and sat opposite each other in the sanctuary. However, as American Methodists prospered, the inconvenience of separating the families became less tolerable. Furthermore, the egalitarian aspect of Methodist camp meetings helped to change the popular attitude towards a more inclusive seating arrangement in chapels. In fact, it was so inclusive that it was an object of criticism by William Annan, a Presbyterian minister.

> Because they [Methodist camp meetings] afford to the mixed multitude who attend them, unusual and most abundant advantages for the practice of wickedness in many of its foulest forms. It is well known that whilst the mass of the steady, orderly, and influential men of the community, who give tone to society, and impart a healthful direction to the current of its manners and customs, take little or no interest in such assemblages [camp meetings], seldom attend, and then for a very short time – on the other hand, persons of almost every shade of color an character are advertised, invited, and expected to attend; and it is of these for the most part that Methodism calculates her gain...Is it the best way to bring together in dangerous combination for many days and nights, men and women in mixed multitudes, where, it cannot be denied, great facilities are presented, to kindle unholy fires in the soul, and practice iniquity in many of is vilest shapes?[219]

Critiques against mixed seating notwithstanding, Methodists were becoming intolerant of the separate seating in their ever-improving houses of worship. About 1830, an alternative seating plan was proposed by Rev. J. Kennaday for a church in Newark. Kennaday's plan permitted men and women to sit in alternating parallel rows separated only by aisles and arranged perpendicular to the altar rail and pulpit. Although the seating arrangement was not readily accepted in Newark, a few years later it was introduced to New York City churches. By 1837, "promiscuous" seating became acceptable in those New York City churches.[220]

The most primitive of Methodist chapels employed simple benches for seating. They were little more that crude wooden planks supported by stumps, barrels, or the most available item. However, as chapels became more sophisticated, they graduated to square pews. These, in turn, were eventually replaced by the more fashionable slip pews. [221]

In 1824, the *Discipline* introduced the rule that churches should be built with free seats.[222] This rule was repeated with each subsequent *Discipline* until 1852. In that edition, the wording was changed to "free seats wherever practicable."[223] Seating became more comfortable and expensive. Unfortunately, it was discovered that the desirable slip pews became a saleable commodity. In an effort to defray construction and operation costs, many churches rented and sold church pews. This was a common practice in many other denominations. For example, historic St. John's Protestant Episcopal Church in Savannah, Georgia was erected in 1853 according to C. N. Otis' High Gothic plan. Their construction cost, originally budgeted for $25,000, rose to $40,000. To cover the shortfall, the church sold their pews at auction for $100 to $500 each.[224]

In New York City, the Protestant Episcopal Church and the Presbyterians dominated the elite classes. High pew prices insured their social exclusivity. In 1852, pew prices were fetching from $100 to $700 plus additional ground rent of 8% per annum.[225]

The sale and rental of pews created no small controversy in the connection. In 1852, the old circuit rider Peter Cartwright called the practice "at war with the best interests of the church" by its degrading treatment of the poor. This was an unexpected causality of the wealth and numerical growth of the MEC. The pew system is inevitably at war with the best interests of the Church, for no honorable, high-minded man, who is poor, and unable to buy or rent a pew, but will feel himself degraded to intrude himself into a pewed church; and that form of worship adopted in any Church which goes to exclude the poor, contravenes the Divine law, and prevents the realization of that blessedness that God has provided for the poor. Fifty years ago there was not a member or preacher among the thousands in the Methodist Episcopal Church that thought of having a pewed church. But since the Church has risen in numerical strength, and become wealthy, this system of pewed churches is fast becoming the order of the day.[226]

In 1863, John E. Risely, a Methodist preacher, observed that because of the pew system the poor "are virtually shut out of the house of God by having a tax imposed upon all the seats, in the form of pew rent, which they are not able to pay; so that supposing they had the disposition to enter these houses of worship, it would be impossible for them to do so."[227] The issue of pew rent was the object of particular scorn for sectarian Benjamin Titus Roberts. Roberts, a pastor of the Genesee Conference, was an avid promoter of Wesleyan perfectionism, abolition, and more stringent discipline. The campaigns for newer and more elaborate church buildings financed by pew money ran contrary to his notion of Methodism as a religion for common folk.[228] By 1860, Roberts publicly denounced the MEC for promoting the alienation of the poorer class by the pew system.

> The pew system, wherever it prevails, not only keeps the masses from attending church, but alienates them, in great degree, from Christianity itself. They look upon it as an institution for the genteel, and the fashionable; and upon Christians as a proud and exclusive class.[229]

That same year Roberts and other like-minded clergy were forced out of the MEC. They re-organized their sect of Free Methodists mostly from the "burned-over district" in upper New York. Roberts charged that the MEC was no longer the same church begun by John Wesley and Francis Asbury. The evidence of this departure from tradition was the apparent deteriorated concern for poor constituents. The formation of the Wesleyan denomination confirmed that the MEC had finally "secularized."[230] However, this does not mean that wealthy churches abandoned the idea that they could help the poor. Rather, it demonstrated that churches justified "excluding the poor from beautiful buildings because the beautiful worshippers were the ones who counted."[231]

Galleries probably developed from rood lofts in sixteenth century English churches. It was primarily used as a place for choirs, musicians, and private seating.[232] They were not unknown in the preaching houses of Wesley's day. Wesley approved of the construction for The New Room in Bristol and the much later City Road Chapel in London. Both were built with gallery seating to accommodate seating and eye contact with the preacher.

The American Methodist experience with chapel galleries has a more ignominious past. In late eighteenth century Delaware, a young African slave by the name of Richard Allen, a member of the "invisible church," was awakened by the preaching of a Methodist itinerant preacher, Rev. Freeborn Garrettson. Inspired to better himself and others, Allen and his brother threw themselves into the backbreaking work of wood splitting as a means to purchase freedom. Not only were they were able to purchase their freedom, but they also accumulated modest personal wealth. Richard Allen's desire to help the local community of African descent led him to consider the options available for free blacks. In 1787, Allen, Absalom Jones and other prominent Africans established the Free African Society in 1787 "for the benefit of each other." He continued social work until 1794 when his church work demanded more attention.[233]

Allen developed quite a reputation as a local preacher for the Methodist Episcopal Church. "Crazy" Lorenzo Dow, the flamboyant Methodist lay preacher, noted that Francis Asbury "jealous of his power, noticed Allen with a watchful eye."[234] Allen was offered the opportunity to travel with Bishop Francis Asbury and "Black Harry" Hosier. Instead, he chose to remain at St. George's Methodist Episcopal Church in Philadelphia. Allen and his associate the Rev. Absalom Jones gathered fellow African Americans for private prayer and Bible study at the predominantly white St. George's. No small controversy occurred over the matter of receiving Holy Communion.

> A number of us usually attended St. George's church in Fourth street; and when the colored people began to get numerous in attending the church, they moved us from the seats we usually sat on, and placed us around the wall, and on Sabbath morning we went to church and the sexton stood at the door, and told us

to go in the gallery. He told us to go, and we would see where to sit. We expected to take the seats over the ones we formerly occupied below, not knowing any better. We took those seats. Meeting had begun, and they were nearly done singing, and just as we got to the seats, the elder said, "Let us pray." We had not been long upon our knees before I heard considerable scuffling and low talking. I raised my head up and saw one of the trustees, H-----M-----, having hold of the Rev. Absalom Jones, pulling him up off of his knees, and saying, "You must get up – you must not kneel here." Mr. Jones replied, "Wait until prayer is over." Mr. H-----M----- said "No, you must get up now, or I will call for aid and force you away." Mr. Jones said, "Wait until prayer is over, and I will get up and trouble you no more." With that he beckoned to one of the other trustees, Mr. L-----S----- to come to his assistance. He came, and went to William White to pull him up. By this time prayer was over, and we all went out of the church in a body, and they were no more plagued with us in the church.[235]

The custom at St. George's was to serve communion to the white members first, while the black members waited in the gallery or some other fringe area.[236] Before St. George's added a second floor gallery, there had been a more egalitarian seating arrangement. At the very least, blacks were allowed to sit in the perimeter on the first floor. The presence of the new gallery changed the spatial dimensions along racial lines without any prior notice to the African members, who were also partakers in funding St. George's.

There is some debate about the historical accuracy of this episode since the gallery was built later. Whatever actually occurred prior, the group staged a walkout from St. George's in 1792.[237] Although they had a substantial spiritual and financial investment into the church, they could not consign themselves to return.

A proposal for a new place of worship was sought. Allen purchased the land on Sixth and Lombard Street that formerly belonged to the Church of England.[238] The building dedication took place on Sunday 29 July 1794. Although Bethel Methodist Church was built as a reaction to racism, worship services there were open to people of all races.

> The Rev. John Dickens sung and prayed, and Bishop Asbury preached. The house was called Bethel, agreeable to the prayer that was made. Mr. Dickens prayed that it might be a bethel to the gathering in of thousands of souls. My dear Lord was with us, so that there were many hearty "amen's" [sic] echoed through the house. This house of worship has been favored with the awakening of many souls, and I trust they are in the Kingdom, both white and colored.[239]

Asbury never mentioned the unfortunate incident at St. George's in his journal. However, he recorded his participation in the dedication service of the new church called Bethel. "I preached at the new African church. Our coloured [sic] brethren are to be governed by the doctrine and discipline of the Methodists."[240] Asbury mentioned Allen specifically only one more time in his journal. Apparently, Allen bought him a fresh horse to continue his long travels.

As early as 1771, Methodists in Georgia were utilizing seating as a means to segregate blacks from whites. They recognized that free seating implied social equality, a difficulty for middle class whites. Blacks were segregated at camp meetings, often behind the preaching stand. In the plain preaching houses whites sat in front benches and blacks in the back. The construction of more elaborate churches initiated the use of galleries for seating blacks.[241]

Wealthy Methodist churches also used the galleries as locations for the organs and choirs. Since the beginning, the use of organs and choirs was the source of no small controversy in Methodist chapels. On the other hand, John Wesley appreciated the aesthetic value of a good pipe organ played well.

> At the cathedral we had a useful sermon, and the whole service was performed with great seriousness and decency. Such an organ I never saw or heard before, so large, beautiful, and so finely toned; and the music of "Glory be to God in the highest," I think exceeded the Messiah itself.[242]

Church organ music reputedly goes back as early as the twelfth century. The first two organs used in America churches were Thomas Brattle's in the Queen's Chapel, Boston, (ca. 1713), and Dean Berkeley's in Trinity Church, Newport, Rhode Island, (ca. 1733).[243]   But it would take considerably more time for organs to enter Methodist chapels. John Wesley greatly appreciated the ascetics of organ music in the Church of England. However, he was reticent to permit them in his chapels. "Let no organ be placed anywhere, till proposed in the Conference."[244]   It had been a favorite instrument of Charles Wesley's sons, Charles and Samuel, who performed their music before social elites and royalty.[245] Samuel Wesley, a renowned organist himself, was said to have been particularly impressed by the singing of the congregants at Leeds. "Those Leeds folks made me play second fiddle."[246]   It is evident that some resistance to organs existed amongst the British Wesleyans from the beginning. Contemporary Daniel Isaac wrote against instruments of all kinds in worship, but especially the organ. "Organs are undoubtedly the worst; because they make most noise, nearly drown the voice of those who sing, and render the words quite inaudible."[247] Thus, the main objection to the organ in the sanctuary was that it distracted from congregational singing, the hallmark of Methodist worship.

Objections aside, the organ became a part of modern worship. British churches that could not afford an organ or musicians were offered "barrel-organs" which could be played simply by turning the crank. Such devices served for up to fifty years in the galleries of British Methodist churches.[248]

In MEC churches, pipe organs were often placed either in the galleries above the entrance or behind the pulpit. The former arrangement created the additional problem of splitting congregation's attention between preacher and musician. Thus, organ music often competed against the pulpit princes in the grand churches. Bangs did not seem to have any particular prejudice against musical instruments. However, he did have an incident in which a fiddler attempted to lure his congregants to dance rather than pray. After a stern public rebuke from Bangs, the "devil's musician" went home and burned his fiddle.[249] His reticence to comment on church organs may be because the topic rivaled the controversy of slavery.[250] Pipe organs and choirs were still controversial until the 1830s. Yet, they both became "omnipresent" as churches increased in wealth.[251]

Historic churches such as John Street and St. George's, not able to change with the times, became more important as remnants of denominational and local history. Surviving "plain and decent" preaching house became either shrines or odd relics of the past. Such shrines were immortalized in legend and verse.

Hail JOHN STREET's venerable shrine!

Hallowed and crowned with joys divine!

At thought of thee what memories rise,

What praise, like incense, fills the skies![252]

The log cabins and meeting houses used by class leaders and circuit riders were snubbed for the more elaborate ambiance of the Greek and Gothic Revival churches. The appendix illustrates the evolution of Methodist churches from the first simple preaching house on John Street to the magnificent neo-Gothic Trinity Methodist Episcopal Church in Manhattan.

Interiors were adorned with fine woods, organs, galleries, and exclusive seating arrangements. Members could now occupy the posh sanctuary seats, insulated from the poorer class, and enjoy worship in a multidimensional experience with a preacher at one end and musicians at the other. Critics of the new form were apt to say, "When I look away to the 'land of steady habits,' where they have pews, and organs, and pay the choir to do their singing – where the itinerant is snugly fixed in the village station, and the local preacher doing what little itinerant work is done, my fears come on."[253] This ever refining worship changed the character of American Methodist life to better serve the more respectable members of the urbane communities.

Stained glass window of Dr. Nathan Bangs from Chapel at Wesleyan University. Note that the artist attempted to correct his posture so that his head and neck would be square with the window.

APPENDIX: Church Architecture in Transition

A: THE FIRST JOHN STREET CHURCH

The first John Street Church building was actually a converted sail-rigging loft. Since church construction was restricted by colonial law, a chimney was added to qualify it as a "residence," ca. 1768.[254]

B: THE SECOND JOHN STREET CHURCH

SECOND JOHN STREET CHURCH.

The second John Street Church was purpose built as "The Model Preaching House" for subsequent Methodist churches, 1818.[255]

C: THE THIRD JOHN STREET CHURCH

Modest Methodist growth was a factor in the Greek Revival construction of the third John Street Church, 1841. [256]

D: TRINITY METHODIST EPISCOPAL CHURCH, NY

Trinity Methodist Episcopal Church - New York, a very prosperous congregation, was one of the first to introduce the lofty Gothic style to American Methodism, ca. 1854.[257]

[1] "A Surprise Party – Compliment to the Rev. Dr. Bangs." *The New York Times.* 24 January 1959. Vol. VIII, no. 2292. Page 1.

[2] Peter Cartwright, *Autobiography of Peter Cartwright,* ed. by Charles L. Wallis, (Nashville: Abingdon Press, 1956, reprint 1984), 148.

[3] William G. McLoughlin, *Revivals, Awakenings, and Reform: An Essay on Religion and Social Change in America, 1607–1977,* (Chicago and London: The University of Chicago Press, 1978), 133.

[4] Philip F. Hardt, *The Soul of Methodism: The Class Meeting in Early New York City Methodism,* (Lanham, New York , and Oxford: University Press of America, 2000), 65.

[5] Stevens, *Life of Bangs,* 207.

[6] John Wesley, "Letter on Preaching Christ," London, December 20, 1751. *Works,* Jackson, XI, 486--487.

[7] Karen B. Westerfield Tucker, *American Methodist Worship,* (New York: Oxford University Press, 2001), 36.

[8] Stevens, *Bangs,* 207.

[9] Russell E. Richey, *Early American Methodism,* (Bloomington and Indiana: Indiana University Press, 1991), 21.

[10] Lester Ruth, *A Little Heaven Below: Worship at Early Methodist Quarterly Meetings,* (Nashville: Kingswood Books, 2000), 189.

[11] Samuel Kennerly to Nathan Bangs, "Work of God on New-River Circuit," *Methodist Review,* 4 (1821): 348.

[12] Maldwyn Edwards, "John Wesley," *A History of the Methodist Church in Great Britain,* Vol. I, general editors Rupert Davies and Gordon Rupp, (London: Epworth Press, 1965), 53.

[13] John Pudney, *John Wesley and His World,* (London: Thames and Hudson, 1978), 82.

[14] George Eayrs, *Wesley and Kingswood and Its Free Churches,* (Bristol: J. W.

Arrowsmith, Ltd., 1911), 46.

[15]Thomas Jackson, *The Life of the Rev. Charles Wesley, M.A.: Some time student of the Christ – Church, Oxford: Comprising a review of his poetry; Sketches of the rise and progress of Methodism; with Notices of contemporary events and characters*, (New York: Published by G. Lane & P. P. Sandford, for the Methodist Episcopal Church, 1842), 156.

[16]Charles Wesley, *The Journal of The Rev. Charles Wesley, M.A.*, edited by Thomas Jackson, vol. I, 1849. (Grand Rapids: Baker Book House, reprint 1980), 151.

[17]Thomas Jackson, *The Life of the Rev. Charles Wesley*, (New York: Published by G. Lane & P. P. Sandford, for the Methodist Episcopal Church, 1842), 156.

[18]Gordon S. Wakefield, *The Spiritual Life in the Methodist Tradition 1791– 1945*, (London: Epworth Press, 1966), 80--81.

[19]Harry S. Stout, *The Divine Dramatist; George Whitefield and the Rise of Modern Evangelicalism*, (Grand Rapids, Michigan: William B. Eerdmans Publishing Company, 1991), 220.

[20]Leigh Eric Schmidt, *Holy Fairs: Scottish Communions and American Revivals in the Early Modern Period*, (Princeton: Princeton University Press, 1989), 3.

[21]Mark A. Noll, *A History of Christianity in the United States and Canada*, (Grand Rapids, Michigan: William B. Eerdmans Publishing Company, 1992), 69.

[22]J. H. S. Burleigh, *A Church History of Scotland*, (London: Oxford University Press, 1960), 292, 293.

[23]Ibid, 293.

[24]George Whitefield to Mr. John Cennick, Glasgow, 16 June 16 1742, *George Whitefield's Letters, from 1734 to 1742*, reprinted from The Works of George Whitefield 1771, (Edinburgh: The Banner of Truth Trust, reprint 1976), 513.

[25]J. H. S. Burleigh, *A Church History of Scotland*, (London: Oxford University Press, 1960), 294.

[26]Leigh Eric Schmidt, *Holy Fairs: Scottish Communions and American Revivals*, (Princeton: Princeton University Press, 1989), 53.

[27]Ibid, 63.

[28]Ibid, 64.

[29]David Purviance, *The Biography of Elder David Purviance*, edited by Levi Purviance, (Dayton: Published for the author by B. F. & G. W. Ellis, 1848), 301.

[30]Barton W. Stone, *The Biography of Elder Barton Warren Stone, written by himself: with Additions and Reflections*, (Cincinnati: American Christian Publications Society, 1853), 35.

[31]Nathan Bangs, *A History of Methodist Episcopal Church*, Vol. II, Third edition, revised and corrected, (New York: Published by G. Lane & C. B. Tippett, 1845), 111--112.

[32]Winthrop S. Hudson and John Corrigan, *Religion in America*, Sixth edition, (Upper Saddle River, New Jersey: Prentice Hall, 1999), 149.

[33]Leigh Eric Schmidt, *Holy Fairs: Scottish Communions and American Revivals in the Early Modern Period*, (Princeton: Princeton University Press, 1989), 60.

[34]Rupert E. Davies, *Methodism*, (London: Epworth Press, 1990), 115--116.

[35]The Wesleyan Conference, *Minutes of the Wesleyan Conference, 1807*: collected edition, ii, 403.

[36]Rupert E. Davies, *Methodism*, (London: Epworth Press, 1990) 116--117.

[37]Lester Ruth, *A Little Heaven Below: Worship at Early Methodist Quarterly Meetings*, (Nashville: Kingswood Books, 2000), 18--19.

[38]Russell E. Richey, *Early American Methodism*, (Bloomington and Indiana: Indiana University Press, 1991), 31.

[39]Lester Ruth, *A Little Heaven Below: Worship at Early Methodist Quarterly Meetings*, (Nashville: Kingswood Books, 2000), 187.

[40]Ibid, 188--189.

[41]Leigh Eric Schmidt, *Holy Fairs: Scottish Communions and American Revivals in the Early Modern Period*, (Princeton: Princeton University Press, 1989), 214.

[42]Joseph Edward Sanderson, *The First Century of Methodism in Canada*, Vol. I 775--1839, (Toronto: William Briggs, 1908), 44--45.

[43]Stevens, *Life of Bangs*, 154--155.

[44]Edmund Storer Janes, *Sermon on the death of Nathan Bangs, D.D.*, (New York: Published by Carlton & Porter, 1862), 20.

[45]Sanderson, *First Century of Methodism in Canada*, Vol. I, 1775--1839, (Toronto: William Briggs, 1908), 45.

[46]Francis Asbury, *Journal of Rev. Francis Asbury*, Vol. III, (New York: Nathan Bangs and Thomas Mason, 1821), 287.

[47]Nathan Bangs, editorial, *Christian Advocate*, (September 9, 1826) quoted in Norman A. McNairn, "Mission to Canada," *Methodist History* XIII (July 1975) No. 4: 58.

[48]John F. Wright, *Sketches of the Life and Labors of James Quinn, who was nearly half a century a minister of the Gospel in The Methodist Episcopal Church.* Cincinnati: Printed at the Methodist Book Concern, for the benefit of the widow, R. P. Thompson, printer, 1851), 181.

[49]Stevens, *Life of Bangs*, 155, 156.

[50]Nathan O. Hatch, *The Democratization of American Christianity*, (New Haven and London: Yale University Press, 1989), 55.

[51]Ann Taves, *Fits, Trances, & Visions: Experiencing Religion and Explaining Experience from Wesley to James*, (Princeton: Princeton University Press, 1999), 235.

[52]Nathan Bangs, "Revival of the work of God in Rhinebeck," *Methodist Review* 4 (May 1821):350, 351.

[53]Nathan O. Hatch, *The Democratization of American Christianity*, (New Haven and London: Yale University Press, 1989), 49.

[54]Abel Stevens, *Essays on the Preaching Required bu the Times and the best methods of*

obtaining it. (New York: Carlton and Phillips, 1856), 125.

[55]DeWitte T. Holland, *The Preaching Tradition: A Brief History,* (Nashville: Abingdon, 1980), 68.

[56]Heman Bangs, *The Autobiography and Journal of Rev. Heman Bangs; with an introduction by Rev. Bishop Janes, D.D.,* edited by his daughters, (New York: N. Tibbals & Son, 1874), 139.

[57]David Lowes Watson, *The Early Methodist Class Meeting,* forward by Albert C. Outler, (Nashville: Discipleship Resources, 1985, reprint 1995), 145.

[58]Ibid, 146--147.

[59]Philip F. Hardt, *The Soul of Methodism: The Class Meeting in Early New York City Methodism,* (Lanham, New York, and Oxford: University Press of America, 2000), 69.

[60]Ann Taves, *Fits, Trances, & Visions: Experiencing Religion and Explaining Experience from Wesley to James,* (Princeton: Princeton University Press, 1999), 235.

[61]Abel Stevens, *Essays on Preaching Required by the Times and the best method of obtaining it.* (New York: Carlton and Phillips, 1856), 151. This book is a compilation of articles originally published in the *National Magazine* (1854) and *Methodist Quarterly Review* (1852).

[62]James Quinn, in *Sketches of the Life and Labors of James Quinn, who was nearly half a century a minister of the Gospel in The Methodist Episcopal Church,* by John F. Wright, (Cincinnati: Printed at the Methodist Book Concern, for the benefit of the widow, R. P. Thompson, Printer, 1851), 260.

[63]L. Dale Patterson, "The Ministerial Mind of American Methodism: The Courses of Study for the Ministry of The Methodist Episcopal Church, The Methodist Episcopal Church, South, and The Methodist Protestant Church: 1880--1920," Dissertation, Drew University, 1984, 56.

[64]John Wesley, "Thoughts on Preaching the Gospel," Reprinted from the *Wesleyan Magazine, Methodist Review* 11 no. 9 (September 1828): 346--348.

[65]Nathan Bangs, *Letters to Young Ministers of the Gospel,* (New York: N. Bangs and J. Emory, 1826), 99.

[66]Nathan Bangs, "Letter to a Junior Preacher," *Methodist Review* 7 March 1824, 114.

[67]William Jay, "Remarks on Preaching," excerpted from the preface of his Lectures abridged and published in the *Wesleyan Methodist Magazine* and reprinted in the *Methodist Review* 10 No. 5 May 1827, 208.

[68]Thomas Maddin, *The Apostate Methodist Preacher*, (Nashville, TN: Published for the author, E. Stevenson & F. A Owen, 1857), 67.

[69]A. Vinet, *Homiletics; or, The Theory of Preaching*, trans. and ed. by Thomas H. Skinner, Third Edition, (New York: Ivison & Phinney; Chicago: S. C. Griggs & Co., 1866), 80. This book was originally published in 1853. Excerpts were published in the *Methodist Quarterly Review* 8 no. 2, April 1854, 303--304. Though it is a bit late for Bangs, it accurately reflects the trend towards didactic preaching at mid-century.

[70]F. R. Webber, *A History of Preaching in Britain and America including the Biographies of Many Princes of the Pulpit and the Men who influenced them*, Part Three, (Milwaukee, WI: Northwestern Publishing House, 1957), 329.

[71]L. Dale Patterson, "The Ministerial Mind of American Methodism: The Courses of Study for the Ministry of The Methodist Episcopal Church, The Methodist Episcopal Church, South, and The Methodist Protestant Church: 1880–1920," Dissertation, Drew University, 1984, 55, 56.

[72]Freeborn Garrettson, *American Methodist Pioneer: The Life and Journals of The Rev. Freeborn Garrettson 1752--1827*, ed. with notes by Robert Drew Simpson, (Rutland, Vermont: Academy Books for Drew University Library, 1984), 399, 400.

[73]Nathan Bangs, *The Life of the Rev. Freeborn Garrettson: compiled from his printed manuscript, journals, and other authentic documents*, (New York: Published by J. Emory and B. Waugh, at the Conference Office, J. Collard, Printer, 1829), 333.

[74]Charles Yrigoyen, Jr., review of *Charles G. Finney and the Spirit of Evangelicalism*, by Charles E. Hambrick-Stowe, *Methodist History* Vol. XXXV (April 1997) No. 3: 200.

[75]Review of, *Lectures on Revivals of Religion* by Charles G. Finney, in *Methodist Review* 30 (July 1848): 477.

[76]Leonard I. Sweet, "The View of Man Inherent in New Measures Revivalism," *Church History* 45 (June 1976): 213.

[77]Ibid, 221.

[78]Horace Bushnell, *Christian Nurture*, (1861; 1888, by Mary A. Bushnell; New Haven:; 1916, by Dotha Bushnell Hillyer; Reprinted by Yale University Press, 1947, 1950, 1953), 9.

[79]Ibid, 64.

[80]Ernest Trice Thompson, *Changing Emphasis in American Preaching: The Stone Lectures for 1943*, (Philadelphia: The Westminster Press, 1943), 21.

[81]Horace Bushnell, *Sermons on Living* Subjects, (1876, Mary A. Bushnell; New York: Charles Scribner's Sons, 1901), 94, *95*.

[82]Joseph Holdich, *The Life of Willbur Fisk, D.D., first president of the Wesleyan University*, (New York: Published by Harper & Brothers, 1842), 332, 333.

[83]Nathan Bangs, *A Discourse on occasion of the death of the Reverend Wilbur Fisk, D.D., president of the Wesleyan University. Delivered in the Greene-Street Church, New-York, on the evening of the 29th of March, 1839*, (New York: Published by the request of those who heard it, Published by T. Mason and G. Lane, for The Methodist Church, at the Conference Office, J. Collard, Printer, 1839), 19.

[84]D. Holmes, *The Methodist Preacher; containing Twenty-eight Sermons, on Doctrinal and Practical Subjects. By Bishop Hedding, Dr. Fisk, Dr. Bangs, Dr. Durbin, and other ministers of The Methodist Episcopal Church*, (Auburn: Derby & Miller: Buffalo: Derby, Orton, & Mulligan, 1853), vi.

[85]During Bangs' brief tenure at Wesleyan University, students were known to imitate his style of elocution. They "unconsciously" mimicked his trademark crook neck and tilted head, due to a condition known as torticollis. Thus, of the four presidential stained glass windows the Memorial Chapel, Bangs' bust was the only one not portrayed in parallel position. Carl F. Price, *Wesleyan's First Century: with an account of the centennial celebration*, (Middletown, CT: Published by Wesleyan University, 1932), 70.

[86]"John P. Durbin, D.D." In *The Illustrated History of Methodism in Great Britain and America, from the days of the Wesleys to the Present Time,* by W. H. Daniels, (New York: Phillips & Hunt: Cincinnati, Chicago, and St. Louis: Walden & Stowe, for the Methodist Book Concern, 1880), 727.

[87]"Bishop Simpson," Ibid, 705.

[88]Paul M. Angle, *"Here I Have Lived": A History of Lincoln's Springfield, 1821--1865,* in *The Lincoln Reader,* ed. by Paul M. Angle, (New York: Rutgers University Press, 1947; Cardinal Giant, 1955), 585–586.

[89]Matthew Simpson, *Lectures on Preaching, delivered before the Theological Department of Yale College,* (New York: Phillips & Hunt; Cincinnati: Hitchcock & Walden, 1879), 98.

[90]Ibid, 304.

[91]Karen B. Westerfield Tucker, *American Methodist Worship,* (Oxford: Oxford University Press, 2001), 38.

[92]Ibid, 39.

[93]Hoyt L. Hickman, *Worshiping with United Methodists: A Guide for Pastors and Church Leaders,* (Nashville: Abingdon Press, 1996), 55.

[94]Hubert Vance Taylor, "Preaching on Slavery, 1831–1861," in *Preaching in American History: selected issues in the American Pulpit, 1630--1967,* ed. by DeWitte Holland, Jess Yoder, and Hubert Vance Taylor, (Nashville and New York: Abingdon Press, 1969), 170, 171.

[95]Typical camp meeting song describing the actual camp meeting scene. Halford Edward Luccock, *The Story of Methodism,* (New York & Cincinnati: Methodist Book Concern, c.1926), 267.

[96]J. Ernest Rattenbury, *Vital Elements of Public Worship,* Third Edition, (London: The Epworth Press, 1936, 1938, 1954), 86.

[97]Charles A. Johnson, *The Frontier Camp Meeting: Religion's Harvest Time,* (Dallas: Southern Methodist University Press, 1955, 1985), 193.

[98]Halford Edward Luccock, *The Story of Methodism,* (New York and Cincinatti:

Methodist Book Concern, c.1926), 267.

[99]Ibid, 267.

[100]Charles A. Johnson, *The Frontier Camp Meeting: Religion's Harvest Time*, (Dallas: Southern Methodist University Press, 1955, 1985), 201.

[101]Hymn I, *Zion's Songster; or, A Collection of Hymns and Spiritual Songs, usually sung at Camp-Meetings, and also in Revivals of Religion*, compiled by Thomas Mason, tenth edition, (New York: J. and J. Harper, Printers, 1835), 1.

[102]James I. Warren, Jr., *O For A Thousand Tongues: The History, Nature, and Influence of Music in the Methodist Tradition*, (Grand Rapids: Francis Asbury Press, 1988), 104--112, *passim*.

[103]Stevens, *Life of Bangs*, 58--59.

[104]John R. Tyson, *Charles Wesley on Sanctification*, (Grand Rapids, Michigan: Francis Asbury Press, 1986), 176.

[105] Stevens, *Life of Bangs*, 351.

[106] John R. Tyson, *Charles Wesley on Sanctification*,(Grand Rapids, Michigan: Francis Asbury Press, 1986), 177.

[107]David Lyle Jeffrey, *English Spirituality in the Age of Wesley*, (Grand Rapids, Michigan: William B. Eerdmans Publishing Company, 1987), 31.

[108]"Forth in thy name, O Lord," in *A Collection of Hymns for the People Called Methodists*, edited by Franz Hildebrandt and Oliver A. Beckerlegge with the assistance of James Dale, The Works of John Wesley, Vol. 7, (Nashville: Abingdon Press, 1983), 470.

[109]Albert C. Outler, ed., *John Wesley*, (New York: Oxford University Press, 1964, 1980), 253.

[110]Stevens, *Life of Bangs*, 396.

[111]Nathan Bangs, *The Necessity, Nature, and Fruits, of Sanctification: in a series of letters to a friend*, (New York: Lane & Scott, Published for the author, 1851).

[112]The popularity of Phoebe Palmer's books and teachings indicate that perfectionist doctrine was actually in demand amongst upwardly mobile urbane Methodists. Kathryn T. Long, "Consecrated Respectability: Phoebe Palmer and the Refinement of American Methodism," *Methodism and the Shaping of American Culture*, ed. by Nathan O. Hatch and John H. Wigger, (Nashville: Kingswood Books, 2001), 284, 285.

[113]Excerpted from the preface of the *Methodist Hymnbook* (1836), in *A History of the Methodist Episcopal Church*, by Nathan Bangs, Vol. III, (New York: T. Mason and G. Lane, 1840), 135.

[114]Nathan Bangs, *Letters to Young Ministers of the Gospel, on the Importance and Method of Study*, (New York: Published by N. Bangs and J. Emory, 1826), 116.

[115] John Lyth, *Glimpses of Early Methodism in York and the Surrounding District*, (York: William Sessions: London: Hamilton, Adams & Co., 1885), 165.

[116]John Wesley, Introduction, *A Collection of Hymns for the Use of the People called Methodists 1780*, edited by Franz Hildebrandt and Oliver A. Beckerlegge with the assistance of James Dale, The Works of John Wesley, Vol. 7, (Nashville: Abingdon Press, 1983), 29.

[117]Ibid, 75.

[118]Lester Ruth, *A Little Heaven Below: Worship at Early Methodist Quarterly Meetings*, (Nashville: Kingswood Books, 2000), 140.

[119]Nathan Bangs, *A History of the Methodist Episcopal Church*, Vol. III, (New York: T. Mason and G. Lane, 1839), 133.

[120]Carlton R. Young, "American Methodist Hymnbooks," in *Companion to the Hymnal: a handbook to the 1964 Methodist Hymnal*, by Fred Gealy, Austin Lovelace, and Carlton Young, (Nashville: New York: Abingdon Press, 1970), 56.

[121]Nathan Bangs, *A History of the Methodist Episcopal Church*, Vol. III, (New York: T. Mason and G. Lane, 1839), 134.

[122]Editorial, *Quarterly Christian Spectator* (September 1829): 521.

[123]Nathan Bangs and Thomas Mason, New York City, to Martin Ruter, Cincinnati,

Ohio, 31 January 1821, Box 18-A, Martin Ruter papers. Archives, Center for Methodist Studies at Bridwell Library, Perkins School of Theology, Southern Methodist University, Dallas.

[124]Nathan Bangs, *The Reviewer Answered: or, The Discipline and Usages of The Methodist Episcopal Church defended against the attacks of The Christian Spectator*, (New York: Published by J. Emory and B. Waugh, 1830), 5.

[125]Preface, *A Collection of Hymns, for the use of the Methodist Episcopal Church, principally from the collection of the Rev. John Wesley, A.M., revised and corrected., with a supplement*, (New York: G. Lane & P.P. Sandford, 1836, 1843), 4.

[126]Ibid, 6.

[127]Robert Guy McCutchan, *Our Hymnody: a manual of The Methodist Hymnal*, Second Edition, (New York: Nashville: Abingdon Press, 1937), 10.

[128]Nathan Bangs, Advertisement to "A Supplement to the Collection of Hymns for the use of The Methodist Episcopal Church, *A Collection of Hymns, for the use of The Methodist Episcopal Church, principally from the collection of the Rev. John Wesley, A.M. Revised and corrected/ With a Supplement*, (New York: Published by G. Lane & P. P. Sandford, For the Methodist Episcopal Church, at the Conference Office, J. Collard, Printer,1843), 527, 528.

[129]Henry Wilder Foote, *Three Centuries of American Hymnody*, (Hamden, CT: Archon Books, 1968.

[130]John Wesley, *A Collection of Hymns for the Use of The People Called Methodists*, The Works of John Wesley, Vol. 7, eds. Franz Hildebrandt and Oliver A. Beckerlegge, (Nashville: Abingdon Press, 1983), 74.

[131]Thomas A. Langford, "Charles Wesley as Theologian," in *Charles Wesley: Poet and Theologian*, ed. by S T Kimbrough, Jr., (Nashville: Kingswood Books, 1992), 99.

[132]Preface, *A Collection of Hymns, for the use of the Methodist Episcopal Church, principally from the collection of the Rev. John Wesley, A.M., revised and corrected., with a supplement*, (New York: G. Lane & P.P. Sandford, 1836, 1843), 4.

[133]Henry Wilder Foote, *Three Centuries of American Hymnody*, (Hamden, CT: Archon Books, 1968), 231.

[134]Stevens, *Life of Bangs*, 347--348.

[135]Ibid, 348.

[136]Robert Emory, *The Life of the Rev. John Emory, one of the Bishops of the Methodist Episcopal Church*, (New York: Published by George Lane for the Methodist Episcopal Church, 1841), 347.

[137]Karen B. Westerfield Tucker, *American Methodist Worship*, (Oxford: Oxford University Press, 2001), 160.

[138]Robert Emory, *The Life of the Rev. John Emory, one of the Bishops of the Methodist Episcopal Church*, (New York: Published by George Lane for the Methodist Episcopal Church, 1841), 347.

[139]*Minutes of Several Conversations between The Rev. Thomas Coke, LL.D. The Rev. Francis Asbury and others, at a Conference, begun in Baltimore, in the State of Maryland, on Monday, the 27th of December, in the Year 1784. Composing a form of Discipline for the Ministers, Preachers and other Members of the Methodist Episcopal Church in America*, (Philadelphia: Printed by Charles Cist, 1785), 22.

[140]*The Doctrines and Discipline of the Methodist Episcopal Church 1856*, (Cincinnati: Published by Swormstedt & Poe, 1856), 81.

[141]Charles D. Cashdollar, *A Spiritual Home: Life in British and American Reformed Congregations, 1830--1915*, (University Park, Pennsylvania: The Pennsylvania State University Press, 2000), 78, 80.

[142]Robert T. Handy, *A History of Union Theological Seminary in New York*, (New York: Columbia University Press, 1987), 41.

[143]Ellouise W. Skinner, *Sacred Music at Union Theological Seminary 1836--1953*, (New York: Union Theological Seminary, 1953), 12 --17, *passim*.

[144]*A Form of Discipline, for the Ministers, Preachers, and Members of the Methodist Episcopal Church in America*, (New York:, 1787), 22.

[145]*The Doctrines and Discipline of the Methodist Episcopal Church 1856*, (Cincinnati: Published by Swormstedt & Poe, 1856), 81.

[146]Ibid, 102--103.

[147]Wesley's rules can be summarized as: 1) sing all; 2) sing lustily; 3) sing modestly; 4) sing in time; and 5) sing spiritually. John Wesley, "Mr. Wesley's Rules for Congregational Singing," reprinted from the *Wesleyan Methodist Magazine*, in *The Methodist Magazine* (May 1824): 189, 190.

[148]Stevens, *Life of Bangs*, 183.

[149]Ibid,185--186.

[150]James F. White, *Protestant Worship: Traditions in Transition*, (Louisville, KY: Westminster/John Knox Press, 1989), 158.

[151]MEC, *Journal of the General Conference, 1820*, (New York: 1820), 239.

[152]MEC, *The Doctrines and Discipline of the Methodist Episcopal Church. The Twenty-Second Edition*, (New York: Published by N. Bangs and J. Emory, for the Methodist Episcopal Church, John C. Totten, Printer, 1824), 72.

[153]James F. White, *Protestant Worship: Traditions in Transition*, (Louisville, KY: Westminister/John Knox Press, 1989), 159.

[154]Stevens, *Life of Bangs*, 168.

[155]Nathan Bangs wrote a series of articles published in *Zion's Herald* and *Western Christian Advocate*. These articles were compiled into a book, *Emancipation*, in which this footnote appears: "According to the statistics of Mexico, lately published, it contains a population of 7,006,000, of whom 4,000,000 are Indians, 2,000,000 mulattoes, 6,000 blacks, and 1,000,000 only are whites; that is, only one-seventh part of the population are whites! And perhaps about the same proportion prevails throughout the South American States; and the successive revolutions show the unsettled habits of the people generally, as well as the unfitness of the ignorant population to govern themselves." *Emancipation; Its Necessity, and Means of Accomplishment: calmly submitted to the Citizens of the United States*, (New York: Published by Lane & Scott, 1849), 36--37.

[156]Wade Crawford Barclay, *History of Methodist Missions, Part Two, The Methodist Episcopal Church 1845–1939*, Vol. III, (New York: The Board of Missions of The Methodist Church, 1957), 176, 177.

[157]Albert J. Raboteau, *Slave Religion: The "Invisible Institution" in the Antebellum South*,

(Oxford: Oxford University Press, 1978, 1980), 318

[158]Thome and Kimball quoted in *The Works of William E. Channing, D.D.*, tenth edition, vol. VI, (Boston: George G. Channing, 1849), 87--88.

[159]John H. Wigger, *Taking Heaven by Storm*, (New York and Oxford: Oxford University Press, 1998), 124.

[160]Randy L. Maddox, "A Change of Affections," in *"Heart Religion" in the Methodist Tradition and Related Movements*, ed. by Richard B. Steele, (Lanham, MD: London: The Scarecrow Press, Inc., 2001), 24.

[161]R. Laurence Moore, *Selling God: American Religion in the Marketplace of Culture*, (New York: Oxford: Oxford University Press, 1994), 78.

[162]Troy Messenger, *Holy Leisure: Recreation and Religion in God's Square Mile*, (Minneapolis and London: University of Minnesota Press, 1999), 12.

[163]Nathan Bangs, *Rites, Ceremonies, and Usages of the Protestant Episcopal Church, tested by Scripture.* (New York: Tract Society of the Methodist Episcopal Church, 183?), 21, 22.

[164]Peter Cartwright, *Autobiography of Peter Cartwright*, (Nashville: Abingdon Press, 1856, Reprint 1956, 1984), 309.

[165]Ibid, 310.

[166]John Bangs, *Autobiography of John Bangs, of the New-York Annual Conference*, (New York: Printed for the Author, 1846),101, 102.

[167]Roman Catholic property values increased threefold by 1860 making it second only to the Methodist Episcopal Church. This does not include the other RC properties such as schools, convents, seminaries, and monasteries. See Jay P. Dolan, *Catholic Revivalism: The American Experience 1830--1900*, (Notre Dame: London: University of Notre Dame Press, 1978), 29.

[168]Nathan Bangs, *The Present State, Prospects, and Responsibilities of the Methodist Episcopal Church*, (New York: Published by Lane & Scott, 1850), 32, 33.

[169]*Minutes of Several Conversations between The Rev. Thomas Coke, LL.D. The Rev. Francis Asbury and others, at a Conference, begun in Baltimore, in the State of Maryland, on*

Monday, the 27th of December, in the Year 1784. Composing a form of Discipline for the Ministers, Preachers and other Members of the Methodist Episcopal Church in America, (Philadelphia: Printed by Charles Cist, 1785), 32.

[170]James Mudge, *History of the New England Conference of the Methodist Episcopal Church 1796--1910*, (Boston: Published by the Conference, 1910), 220, 221.

[171]Vestry Street, Mulberry Street, and Forty-first Street moved uptown in 1833, 1835, and 1846, respectively. Madison Street and Cherry Street merged in 1844. The church-ship "John Wesley," a ministry to seamen, was replaced by Bethel ship after 1854. J. B. Wakeley, *Lost Chapters recovered from The Early History of American Methodism*, (New York: Published for the author, 1858), 589.

[172]Douglass C. North, *The Economic Growth of the United States 1790--1860*, (New York: W. W. Norton & Company, Inc., 1961, 1966.), 198.

[173]Stevens, *Life of Bangs*, 204, 205.

[174]Lewis R. Streeter, *Past and Present of the John Street Methodist Episcopal Church New York* (New York: by the Pastor, 1913), 24.

[175]Most MEC's were built or rebuilt in Greek Revival from 1820 to 1850, with the exception of some Greek mixed with Gothic towards the end of this period. Andrew Landale Drummond, *The Church Architecture of Protestantism: An Historical and Constructive Study*, (Edinburgh: T & T Clark, 1934), 58 --60.

[176]Nathan Bangs, *The Substance of A Sermon preached on opening the Methodist Church in John-street, in the city of New York, on the morning of the 4th of January, 1818*, (New York: Published at the request of the Trustees of said Church, Printed by John C. Totten, 1818), 19, 20.

[177]Joshua Soule, *The Substance of a Discourse, delivered in the New Methodist Meeting House in John-street, New-York: On the Evening of the 4th of January, 1818; being the day on which said house was opened for Divine Worship*, (New York: Published by request of the Trustees of the Church, Printed by John C. Totten, 1818), 24, 25.

[178]Joshua Soule, *Object and Nature of Religious Worship: A Discourse delivered at the dedication of John-Street Church, New York, Jan. 4, 1818*, (Nashville: Published

by E. Stevenson & F. A. Owen, Agents, for The Methodist Episcopal Church, South, 1857).

[179]Stevens, *Life of Bangs*, 225.

[180]Ibid, 225--226.

[181]Lewis R. Streeter, *Past and Present of the John Street Methodist Episcopal Church, (First Methodist Society in America) New York, Including Earliest and Latest Methodist Edifices in London*, (New York: 1913), 25.

[182]Aymar Embury II, *Early American Churches*, (Garden City, New York: Doubleday, Page & Company, 1914), 138.

[183]John Holland, *Memoirs of the Life and Ministry of Rev. John Summerfield, A.M.*, seventh edition, (New York: Published by J. K. Wellman, 1845), 332, 333.

[184]Ibid, 334, 335.

[185]Catherine A. Brekus, *Strangers and Pilgrims: Female Preaching in America, 1740--1845*, (Chapel Hill: University of North Carolina Press, 1998), 285.

[186]Karen B. Westerfield Tucker, *American Methodist Worship*, (Oxford: Oxford University Press, 2001), 247.

[187]Samuel A. Seaman, *A History of Methodism in New York City*, (New York: Hunt & Eaton: Cincinnati: Cranston & Stowe, 1892), 323--325.

[188]William James, *The Varieties of Religious Experience: A Study in Human Nature being the Gifford Lectures on Natural Religion delivered at Edinburgh in 1901--1902*, (New York: The New American Library of World Literature, Inc., 1958), 349.

[189]Wayne Andrews, *Architecture, Ambition, and Americans: A Social History of American Architecture*, revised edition, (New York: The Free Press, 1978), 71, 72.

[190]Andrew Landale Drummond, *The Church Architecture of Protestantism: An Historical and Constructive Study*, (Edinburgh: T & T Clark, 1934), 58.

[191]Phoebe B. Stanton, *The Gothic Revival & American Church Architecture: An Episode in Taste 1840--1856*, Baltimore and London: The Johns Hopkins University

Press, 1968, 1997), 20, 21.

[192]William H. Willimon, *Word, Water, Wine and Bread: How Worship Has Changed over the Years*, (Valley Forge: Judson Press, 1980), 110, 111.

[193]Basil F. L. Clarke, *Church Builders of the Nineteenth Century: A Study in The Gothic Revival in England*, (London: Society for Promoting Christian Knowledge; New York: The MacMillan Company, 1938), 74, 75.

[194]Basil F. L. Clarke, *Church Builders of the Nineteenth Century: A Study in The Gothic Revival in England*, (London: Society for Promoting Christian Knowledge; New York: The MacMillan Company, 1938), 74, 75.

[195]James F. White, *The Cambridge Movement: The Ecclesiologists and the Gothic Revival*, Cambridge: Cambridge at the University Press, 1962), 180.

[196]Phoebe Stanton, *The Gothic Revival & American Church Architecture: An Episode in Taste 1840--1856* (Baltimore: The John Hopkins Press, 1968, 1997), 59.

[197]John Summerson, *Heavenly Mansions and other Essays on Architecture*, (New York: W. W. Norton & Company, Inc., 1963), 173.

[198]Phoebe B. Stanton, *The Gothic Revival & American Church Architecture: An Episode in Taste 1840--1856* (Baltimore: The John Hopkins Press, 1968, 1997), 216--219.

[199]Barton Brown, "Quest for the Temple: A study of the New York Ecclesiological Society 1848--1855 and its effect upon the architectural setting of worship in the Episcopal Church in the United States of America 1840--1860," (Master of Sacred Theology thesis, General Theological Seminary, 1968), 13.

[200]Peter F. Anson, *Fashions in Church Furnishings 1840--1940*, (London: The Faith Press, 1960), 68.

[201]Andrew Landale Drummond, *The Church Architecture of Protestantism: An historical and constructive study*, (Edinburgh: T & T Clark, 1934), 90.

[202]Jeanne Halgren Kilde, *When Church Became Theatre: The Transformation of Evangelical Architecture and Worship in Nineteenth-Century America*, (Oxford: Oxford University Press, 2002), 57, 58.

[203] Frank L. Greenagel, *The New Jersey Churchscape: Encountering Eighteenth and Nineteenth Century Churches*, (New Brunswick, NJ: Rutgers University Press, 2001), 30.

[204] Vicki Bennett, *Sacred Space and Structural Style: The Embodiment of Socio-religious Ideology*, (Ottawa: University of Ottawa Press, 1997), 219.

[205] H. N. McTyeire, editorial, "Houses for Worship," *Christian Advocate*, Thursday February 3, 1859, Vol. 23, No 5.

[206] "Pittsburgh," *Cyclopaedia of Methodism*, ed. Matthew Simpson, (Philadelphia: Everts & Stewart, 1876, 1878), 722.

[207] Donald B. Marti, "Rich Methodists: The Rise and Consequences of Lay Philanthropy in the Mid-Nineteenth Century," *Perspectives on American Methodism: Interpretive Essays*, ed. by Russell E. Richey, Kenneth E. Rowe, and Jean Miller Schmidt, (Nashville: Kingswood Books, 1993), 266.

[208] Kenneth E. Rowe, "Redesigning Methodist Churches: Auditorium-Style Sanctuaries and Akron-Plan Sunday Schools in Romanesque Costume 1875--1925," *Connectionalism: Ecclesiology, Mission and Identity*, eds. Russell E. Richey, Dennis M. Campbell, and William B. Lawrence, (Nashville: Abingdon Press, c.1997), 118.

[209] Anne C. Loveland and Otis B. Wheeler, *From Meetinghouse to Megachurch: A Material and Cultural History*, (Columbia and London: University of Missouri Press, 2003), 26, 27.

[210] Charles Grandison Finney, *Memoirs of Rev. Charles G. Finney*, (New York: A.S. Barnes & Company, 1876), 323, 324, 325.

[211] Ibid, 326.

[212] Stevens, *Life of Bangs*, 292.

[213] Report of the Committee on the Memorial from Washington City, *Journal of the General Conference, 1852* in *Journals of the General Conference of the Methodist Episcopal Church*, Vol. III, 1848--1856, (New York: Carlton & Lanahan; San Francisco: E. Thomas; Cincinnati: Hitchcock & Walden, n.d.), 202.

[214] Stevens claimed that Bangs was the "chief actor in the most important measures

of" all except one General Conferences from 1808 to 1852. Stevens, *Life of Bangs*, 380.

[215]Lillian Brooks Brown, *A Living Centennial Commemorating the One Hundredth Anniversary of Metropolitan Memorial United Methodist Church*, (Washington, District of Columbia: 1969), 7. See illustration in Appendix.

[216]Nathan Bangs, "Rise and progress of the Methodist Episcopal Church in New-Haven, Connecticut," *Methodist Review* 10 no. 6 June 1827, 265.

[217]*Minutes of Several Conversations between The Rev. Thomas Coke, LL.D. The Rev. Francis Asbury and others, at a Conference, begun in Baltimore, in the State of Maryland, on Monday, the 27th of December, in the Year 1784. Composing a form of Discipline for the Ministers, Preachers and other Members of the Methodist Episcopal Church in America*, (Philadelphia: Printed by Charles Cist, 1785), 32.

[218]John Wesley, "Minutes of Several Conversations," *Works*, Jackson edition, Vol. III, 332.

[219]Interesting to note that the book was endorsed by Archibald Alexander, President of Princeton Seminary. William Annan, *The Difficulties of Arminian Methodism; embracing Strictures on the Writings of Wesley, Dr. Clarke, Fisk, Bangs, and others, in a series of letters addressed to the Rev. ****,* (Pittsburgh: Published by Luke Loomis; 1838), 203,204.

[220]Samuel A. Seaman, *Annals of New York Methodism, being a History of the Methodist Episcopal Church in the City of New York from A.D. 1766 to A.D. 1890*, (New York: Hunt and Eaton: Cincinnati: Cranston & Stowe, 1892), 268, 269.

[221]Aymar Embury II, *Early American Churches*, (Garden City, New York: Doubleday, Page & Company, 1914), 138.

[222]*The Doctrines and Discipline of the Methodist Episcopal Church the Twenty-Second Edition*, (New York: Published by N. Bangs and J. Emory, John C. Totten, Printer, 1824),160.

[223]*The Doctrines and Discipline of the Methodist Episcopal Church 1856*, (Cincinnati: Published by Swormstedt and Poe, 1856), 169.

[224]Eight pews, four each, were later set aside as free seats for black and poor white members. Linton Weeks, *St. John's Church in Savannah*, (Savannah,

Georgia: St. John's Church, 1985), 21, 24.

[225]Sven Beckert, *The Monied Metropolis: New York City and the Consolidation of the American Bourgeoisie, 1850--1896*, (Cambridge: New York: Cambridge University Press, 1993, 2001, 2003), 59.

[226]Peter Cartwright, *Autobiography of Peter Cartwright*, reprint 1856, (Nashville: Abingdon Press, 1956, 1984), 312--313.

[227]John E. Risely, *Some Experiences of a Methodist Itinerant, in a ministry of half a century*, (Boston: Printed for the Author, 1882), 122, 123.

[228]Melvin E. Dieter, *The Holiness Revival of the Nineteenth Century*, second edition, (Lanham, Md, and London: The Scarecrow Press, Inc., 1996), 45--46.

[229]Benjamin T. Roberts, *The Methodist Experience in America: A Sourcebook*, Vol II, edited by Russell E. Richey, Kenneth E. Rowe, and Jean Miller Schmidt, (Nashville: Abingdon Press, 2000), 320.

[230]Roger Finke and Rodney Stark, *The Churching of America, 1776--1990: Winners and Losers in our Religious Economy*, (New Brunswick, New Jersey: Rutgers University Press, 1992, 2000), 153.

[231]Richard L. Bushman, *The Refinement of America: Persons, Houses, Cities*, (New York: Vintage Books, 1992, 1993), 352.

[232]Francis Bond, *Screens and Galleries in English Churches*, (Oxford: London: New York: Toronto: Oxford University Press, 1908), 149.

[233]E. Curtis Alexander, *Richard Allen: The First Exemplar of African American Education*, (New York: ECA Associates, 1985), 78--79.

[234]Lorenzo Dow quoted in George A. Singleton, *The Romance of African Methodism: A Study of the African Methodist Episcopal Church*, (New York: Exposition Press, 1952), 9.

[235]Richard Allen, *The Life Experience and Gospel Labors of the Rt. Rev. Richard Allen*, Bicentennial edition, (Nashville: Abingdon Press, 1983), 25.

[236]George A. Singleton, *The Romance of African Methodism: A Study of the African Methodist Episcopal Church*, (New York: Exposition Press, 1952), 9.

[237]James Varick led a similar walkout from John Street Church in 1796. In 1821 he organized and founded the African Methodist Episcopal Church, Zion. The Colored Methodist Episcopal Church (now Christian Methodist Episcopal Church) grew out of the "colored" conferences of the Methodist Episcopal Church, South in 1870.

[238]Richard Allen, *The Life Experience and Gospel Labors of the Rt. Rev. Richard Allen*, Bicentennial edition, (Nashville: Abingdon Press, 1983), 31.

[239]Ibid, 31.

[240]Francis Asbury, *Journal of Rev. Francis Asbury*, Vol. II, (New York: Lane & Scott, 1852), 231.

[241]Christopher H. Owen, *The Sacred Flame of Love: Methodism and Society in Nineteenth-Century Georgia*, (Athens and London: The University of Georgia Press, 1998), 17, 18.

[242]John Wesley, Journal August 29, 1762, *Works*, Jackson edition, vol. III, 111.

[243]Aubrey Thompson-Allen, "The History of the Organ," *Religion in Life*, Vol. XXIV Winter, 1954--55 No. 1, 136

[244]John Wesley, "Several Conversations," *Works*, Jackson edition, vol. VIII, 319.

[245]Philip Olleson, "The Wesleys at Home: Charles Wesley and His Children," *Methodist History* vol. XXXVI April 1998 no. 3, 139--158, *passim*.

[246]Benjamin Gregory, *Side Lights on the Conflicts of Methodism during the Second Quarter of the Nineteenth Century 1827--1852*, (London, Paris, New York and Melbourne: Cassell and Company, Limited, 1899), 63.

[247]Daniel Isaac, *Vocal Melody; or, Singing the only music sanctioned by Divine Authority, in the Public Worship of Christians*, (York: Printed by Richard Burdekin, 1827), v.

[248]W. T. Whitely, *Congregational Hymn-Singing*, (London: J. M. Dent & Sons Ltd., 1933), 149, 150.

[249]Stevens, *Life of Bangs*, 104.

[250]Ibid, 316.

[251]James F. White, *Introduction to Christian Worship*, Third edition, revised and expanded, 2000), 126.

[252]Excerpted from George Lansing Taylor, "A Centennial Rhyme," in Daniel Wise, *1866. The Children's Centenary Memorial*, (New York: N. Tibbals, 1866), 114.

[253]Anonymous letter to John F. Wright, in *Sketches of the Life and Labors of James Quinn, who was nearly half a century a minister of the Gospel in The Methodist Episcopal Church*, (Cincinnati: Printed at the Methodist Book Concern, for the benefit of the widow, R. P. Thompson, Printer, 1851), 267.

[254] J.B. J.B. Wakely, *Lost Chapters recovered from The Early History of American Methodism*, (New York: published by the author, by Carlton & Porter, 1858), 108.

[255] J.B. Wakely, 580.

[256] J. B. Wakely, 584.

[257] J.B. Wakley, 588.

ABOUT THE AUTHOR

Daniel F. Flores is an Elder in the Rio Texas Conference of The United Methodist Church. He holds the following earned degrees: B.A. in Bible, Southeastern College; M.A. in Theology, Gordon-Conwell Theological Seminary; M.Div., Princeton Theological Seminary; M.S. in Library and Information Science, Drexel University; M.Phil. and Ph.D. in Theological & Religious Studies with a concentration in American Religion & Culture, Drew University. He is married to Rev. Thelma Herrera Flores, an ordained United Methodist Deacon.

Made in the USA
Columbia, SC
30 October 2024

45270543R00069